ii

Hamilton's Women

Other Works by Valerie Estelle Frankel

Henry Potty and the Pet Rock: A Harry Potter Parody
Henry Potty and the Deathly Paper Shortage: A Harry Potter Parody
Buffy and the Heroine's Journey
From Girl to Goddess: The Heroine's Journey in Myth and Legend
Katniss the Cattail: The Unauthorized Guide to Name and Symbols
The Many Faces of Katniss Everdeen: The Heroine of The Hunger Games
Harry Potter, Still Recruiting: A Look at Harry Potter Fandom
Teaching with Harry Potter
An Unexpected Parody: The Spoof of The Hobbit Movie
Teaching with Harry Potter
Myths and Motifs in The Mortal Instruments
Winning the Game of Thrones: The Host of Characters & their Agendas
Winter is Coming: Symbols and Hidden Meanings in A Game of Thrones
The Girl's Guide to the Heroine's Journey
Choosing to be Insurgent or Allegiant: Symbols, Themes & Analysis of the Divergent Trilogy
Doctor Who and the Hero's Journey
Doctor Who: The What Where and How
Sherlock: Every Canon Reference You May Have Missed in BBC's Series
Symbols in Game of Thrones
How Game of Thrones Will End
Joss Whedon's Names
Pop Culture in the Whedonverse
Women in Game of Thrones: Power, Conformity, and Resistance
History, Homages and the Highlands: An Outlander Guide
The Catch-Up Guide to Doctor Who
Remember All Their Faces: A Deeper Look at Character, Gender and the Prison World of Orange Is The New Black
Everything I Learned in Life I Know from Joss Whedon
Empowered: The Symbolism, Feminism, & Superheroism of Wonder Woman
The Avengers Face their Dark Sides
The Comics of Joss Whedon: Critical Essays
Mythology in Game of Thrones
We're Home: Fandom, Fun, and Homages in Star Wars the Force Awakens
The English Teacher's Guide to the Hamilton Musical: Symbols, Allegory, Metafiction, and Clever Language
Who Tells Your Story?: History, Pop Culture, and Hidden Meanings in the Musical Phenomenon Hamilton

Hamilton's Women

Revolutionary Heroines of the Musical Phenomenon

Valerie Estelle Frankel

Hamilton's Women is an unauthorized guide to the *Hamilton* musical and related works. None of the individuals or companies associated with this series or any merchandise based on this series has in any way sponsored, approved, endorsed, or authorized this book.

Copyright © 2019 Valerie Estelle Frankel
All rights reserved.
LitCrit Press

ISBN: 9781086073089

CONTENTS

Introduction 9
PART I: Alexander's Family 11
  Mrs. Hamilton...12
  Mrs. Schuyler..15
  The Schuyler Sisters..19
  Angelica's Marriage...25
  Angelica and Hamilton.......................................33
  The Love Triangle 38
  Eliza's Childhood 45
  Courting Eliza 47
  Eliza as Wife and Founding Mother.................55
  Eliza's Legacy..67
  Peggy...72
  Maria Reynolds..78
PART II: The Unseen Women 89
  Mrs. Burr..91
  Theodosia I and her Mark on History.............93
  Theodosia II..99
  Sally Hemings...106
  Martha Washington..110
  Abigail Adams...112
  Dolley Madison...114
  The Bullet...115
  The Stories that Aren't Told: Ensemble...........118
Conclusion 125
Appendix..127
  Songs..129
  Original Cast and Creators 2015-2016 131
  Works Cited 132

VALERIE ESTELLE FRANKEL

Introduction

For characters with such small roles in a male-bonding musical, the women of *Hamilton* are striking. Angelica, Eliza...and Peggy defiantly explore New York, singing of how the city and America's future is theirs. Next comes Eliza's romance with Hamilton, spinning straight from meeting to courtship and wedding in a flurry of letters and dizzying whirls. Breaking with musical convention, their arc then rewinds on the turntable stage to reveal a very different account of the romance from Angelica's point of view.

His wife and sister-in-law continue balancing Hamilton through the rest of the story. Even as the two women support him, they also battle with him over the fate of the country and the "narrative" he is shaping with his legacy. Each guides him, one as an intellectual muse and the other as his true love. At the same time, they are far from passive, and they don't hesitate to show him his wrongness when needed.

Next comes Maria the bad girl, played by Peggy's actress and emphasizing the good girl/bad girl split so common to musicals. Maria is more cliché than character as Hamilton succumbs to her seductive (but naïve!) wiles and is destroyed. So much for the show's women. Still, among the ensemble,

Sally Hemings, Mrs. Hamilton, and even the Bullet nod to the less-seen heroines in the story. Onstage, women play soldiers, spies, and duelists, saluting the roles historical women played in the Revolution, even as they make visual strides toward a more egalitarian future. More famous historical figures also are acknowledged as they impact the central heroes—in particular, the country's Founding Mothers, Mrs. Theodosia Burr and her daughter Theodosia Burr Alston.

Of course, creator Lin-Manuel Miranda was limited in how much he could include. Scenes following Ben Franklin and John Adams as well as depicting Theodosia's death and her daughter's accomplishments soon hit the cutting-room floor. Great moments from history, like Peggy's dodging a tomahawk to rescue her baby sister, Dolley Madison's creating the role of First Lady during Jefferson's reign, Theodosia's uncovering Benedict Arnold's treachery, and Aaron Burr's plotting to make his daughter queen of Mexico didn't make it in. There's an incredible richness to these women's lives, even as they shaped the country's history. Here are all these stories—the great moments that shaped the show's heroines in history and consideration of their roles in the musical as they take control of a narrative that was never just about Founding Fathers.

PART I:
Alexander's Family

MRS. HAMILTON

The first woman described in the show has a foundational effect on young Alexander Hamilton, as it's his beloved mother. As Thomas Fleming explains in his book, *The Intimate Lives of the Founding Fathers:*

> Marital turmoil seems to have been endemic in Alexander Hamilton's family. His maternal grandmother, Mary Uppington Fawcett, separated from her dour, aging husband, Dr. John Fawcett, and moved from the West Indian island of Nevis to neighboring St. Kitts with her only surviving child, Rachel. Mary must have been extremely unhappy; she gave up her rights to Dr. Fawcett's considerable estate in return for fifty-three pounds and four shillings in annual support. Rachel Fawcett matured into a beautiful and spirited woman and proceeded to replicate her mother's history—and then some. (209)

Rachel Faucette had been born in Nevis and lived on St. Croix. Hamilton described his mother as "a handsome young woman with a snug fortune" before meeting his first husband, according to Ron Chernow's famous biography that inspired the musical (10). Indeed, she had a large inherence from her father, before her husband squandered it. "In 1745, Rachel and her mother moved to the Danish-owned island of St. Croix, where at age sixteen Rachel married twenty-eight-year-old John Michael Lavien, a merchant with a murky background and a fondness for splendid clothes. Lavien seemed rich. Apparently he thought Rachel, who had inherited some St. Croix property in her father's will, was also rich" (Fleming 209). Alexander insists she married the rich-appearing (though actually impoverished) man "in compliance with the wishes of her mother...but against her own inclination" (Chernow 10). He adds that it soon became "a hated mar-

HAMILTON'S WOMEN

riage" (10).

He was a clothing merchant, and they had a son, Peter, in 1746. However, as he lost all her wealth, she left him in disgust. Chernow insists there is no evidence she turned to prostitution—a slander spread repeatedly by Lavien—though she may have had affairs (11). For his vengeance, Lavien shockingly had her locked in a St. Croix prison most often used to torture rebellious slaves. Once out, she ran away with her mother, abandoning Lavien and four-year-old Peter.

On St. Kitts, she fell in love with James Hamilton, a Scottish lord's younger son and agent for a Glasgow tobacco merchant, and had two surviving sons with him, James Jr. and Alexander. They moved from island to island, seeking money and the chance to shake off condemnation for bigamy. She and Lavien officially divorced in 1759, but Lavien officially described her as "having shown herself to be shameless, rude and ungodly ... and given herself up to whoring with everyone." Moreover, Lavien termed Alexander and his brother "whore-children" and persuaded the court to rule that they could never inherit his property (Fleming 210). By the terms, she was not free to remarry—her children were legally bastards and would be forever.

> James was a handsome, charming loser who virtually specialized in going bankrupt. Rachel and James Hamilton soon moved to nearby Nevis, the tiny island of her birth, and for the next fourteen or fifteen years lived a precarious existence punctuated by Hamilton's various attempts to make money as a merchant, all of which ended in disaster. In keeping with the relaxed sexual mores of the West Indies, there is no record of a formal marriage. (Fleming 210)

The family managed, but hardly thrived, with their very existence and insult to social mores of the time. "A pregnancy could doom a woman to a life on the streets characterized by poverty, prostitution, and an early death. Nowhere is an example of this more clear and poignant than Alexander's own mother's life," notes feminist scholar Catherine Allgor (100). Still, the show dismisses most of this, and Rachel's struggle to succeed, to change the focus to her sons' illegitimacy and their loss of both parents.

Soon enough, James went on a business trip and did not return. As an adult, Alexander forgivingly writes to his brother James, "But what has become of our dear father? It is an age since I have heard from him or of him...My heart bleeds at the recollection of his misfortunes and embarassments" (Villegas 85). He appears to have believed his father's desertion to be a noble act. Further, "In the tens of thousands of words Hamilton wrote in his hyperactive life, he never mentioned his mother with affection. On the contrary, when he was about to marry, he felt compelled to ask his fiancée if she would share 'every kind of fortune with him.' He attributed his anxiety to his experience with 'a female heart' who declined to tolerate a husband's failure," as Fleming decides (211).

Whatever her failings, Rachel appears to have done her best for the boys. "Rachel tried to give her spartan household a patina of civility. From a later inventory, we know that she had six silver spoons, seven silver teaspoons, a pair of sugar tongs, fourteen porcelain plates, two porcelain basins, and a bed covered with a feather comforter" (Chernow 24). She and her boys lived on the top floor and kept a goat in the yard, while the ground floor was a shop selling food to planters—though "it was uncommon in those days for a woman to be a shopkeeper, especially one so fetching and, at thirty-six, still relatively young" (Chernow 23). This emphasizes her independence as a single mother, determined to preserve her family.

On the show, the future Mrs. Hamilton, Eliza, fills in for Alexander's mother and tells her part of the exposition in the first number: This emphasizes her role as eventual storyteller, bookending her place in the narrative and also emphasizing how she will become his new family: "When he was ten his father split, full of it, debt-ridden/Two years later, see Alex and his mother bed-ridden/Half-dead sittin' in their own sick, the scent thick," she narrates. This indeed was Rachel's fate, condemning her sons to destitution. On her death, her property went to the legitimate son, Peter, and Alexander and his full brother had to find work at their tender ages.

Throughout the show, Hamilton continues mentioning her, remembering her sadly as his last vestige of a happy family when he proposes to Eliza in "Helpless," and remembering the tragedy of her death and his own near-death during the song "Hurricane."

In his final monologue, Alex acknowledges his mother as "waiting...on the other side" in a source of comfort. In this, she fulfils the traditional fairytale role of the saintly dead mother, whose loss propels the hero out on his journey without her protection, only with the memory of her perfect love. With this, Rachel and her influence on the story are more stereotype than character. She loved and shaped Hamilton, but never stands out in the show.

MRS. SCHUYLER

Puzzlingly, only Eliza's father appears on the show, though her mother was also living at the time of her marriage. Admittedly, the father functions in the story as an important obstacle who can accept or refuse Hamilton as suitor (and walks in on his embarrassing dance of triumph after he wins her hand). Having two parents do so would add an unneeded character and not alter the story. While Eliza's father gives her away at the wedding, having a mother there beside the two sisters is not especially vital visually.

However, historically, Kitty Schuyler was very much a part of this narrative as, in reality, the general was pleased with Alexander but insisted he would only give permission for the marriage if his wife agreed. "Men may have ruled over women as a matter of law in the eighteenth century, but Philip and Kitty Schuyler enjoyed a long and happy marriage, in part because he did not undercut her household authority as either mistress or mother," Eliza's biographer Tilar J. Mazzeo explains of this twist (75). Kitty had not met Alexander and took a suspenseful month to give her consent. At last, permission came, but both parents were eager to marry Eliza off properly at their own home, with all the neighbors invited and the traditional celebration given. The wedding was set for nearly a year later. When she agreed, Hamilton wrote a flattering letter to Mrs. Schuyler, adding, "May I hope, madam, you will not consider it as a mere profession when I add that, though I have not the happiness of a personal acquaintance with you, I am no stranger to the qualities that distinguish your character and these make the relation in which I stand to you not one of the least pleasing circumstances of my union with your daughter" (Chernow 136).

Philip and Catherine Schuyler had married in 1755, when she was twenty. They had fifteen children together, eight of whom survived to adulthood. Thanks to her position, she was a representative figure in her Dutch colony and among the women of the Revolution. "In her own character she was so domestic, retiring, and unobstrusive that many of the details of her life can only be discovered indirectly and with difficulty," as Mary Gay Humphreys reveals in her century-old biography *Catherine Schuyler,* filled with details of upstate New York (v). She had an eventful life on the farm: "By twenty-nine, Kitty Schuyler had given birth to six children and buried half of them" (Mazzeo 12). On the frontier, this was a great burden, as were the many other trivialities of daily life on a complex farm.

Major General Philip Schuyler "was one of the richest men in America, owner of great swaths of land along the Mohawk and Hudson rivers" (Fleming 220). He also had one of the greatest law libraries in New York, where young husband Hamilton and family friend Aaron Burr with studied to pass the bar. Kitty tended her husband the general and his men during the French and Indian War. While he was off at battle, she raised her three small daughters in her mother-in-law's home, and then finally designed and built a Georgian brick mansion for her family on the Hudson River with an elegant ballroom, "still standing at the head of Schuyler Street, Albany, and now the home of the Sisters of St. Francis de Sales" (Humphreys 64-65). Elizabeth and Alexander were married there as was Mrs. McIntosh, the owner of the time, to President Millard Fillmore. "Kitty also built the estate they called 'the Pastures' to be a veritable fortress. She was no stranger to war. The walls were thickened to withstand attacks, and the doors fitted with brass locks and heavy brackets," Mazzeo explains (10). Eventually, these came to save Eliza and her family. As the Revolutionary War went on, armed guards had to patrol their manor and there were repeated assassination attempts, from British-allied Iroquois as well as the British themselves.

When her husband was injured in battle, Kitty went to him and nursed him in Ticonderoga until his recovery. Danger then came to their home, as the local Iroquois plotted to burn down the home in Saratoga and kill everyone within. However, their leader, who had been a well-treated guest there, relented, saying, "I have eaten his bread. I cannot kill him" (Humphreys 146). Their hospitality had indeed saved their lives.

Along with the Pastures, "The enterprising Schuyler also built a two-story house on the fringe of the Saratoga wilderness, where he created an industrial village with four water-power mills, a smithy, and storehouses that employed hundreds of people" (Chernow 135). Kitty raced there on horseback to save the silver, horses, and other valuables, even after a neighbor was scalped by an alliance of Tories. "Putting aside entreaties and tales of danger, she set out on her perilous journey from Albany accompanied by only one armed man" as the others were needed as soldiers (Humphreys 153-154). When people on the road urged her to turn back, she retorted, "A general's wife should not know fear" (Humphreys 154). She arrived safely, only to receive a startling letter from her husband. As the British were coming, she must torch the fields, destroying the crops they had worked all year to grow. This she did, in a bold example to her neighbors. "A century later, when people came to tell the story of small acts that helped to win the American Revolution, the tale of Catherine Schuyler burning her fields was still being repeated and depicted in illustrations" (Mazzeo 52). She then retrieved her valuables and fled. In fact, General John Burgoyne's forces soon took control of the house in Saratoga and finally burned it down in September 1777.

Later, Kitty endured further indignity when her husband magnanimously invited that same General Burgoyne to stay with them when he had been captured by the American forces. As the general's wife recorded in her letters:

> We were received by the Good General Schuyler, his wife and daughters, not as enemies but as kind friends; and they treated us with the most marked politeness, as they did General Burgoyne who had caused their beautifully finished house to be burned. In fact they all behaved like persons of exalted minds, who determined to bury all recollections of their own injuries in contemplation of our misfortunes. General Burgoyne was struck with General Schuyler's generosity and said to him "You show us great kindness, though I have done you so much injury." "That was the fate of war," replied the brave man. "Let us say no more about it." (Humphreys 159).

Later that year, he began rebuilding on the same site, now maintained by the National Park Service. Rebuilt by Philip and Kitty, it evolved into the village of Schuylerville.

Since all the family slaves were descended from two women, their contributions to the household should be mentioned. Mrs. Grant, writing about life at the time, accounts for the "rivalries in excellence" between the two families. "Diana was determined that in no respect of excellence Maria's children should surpass hers; and Maria was equally determined that Diana's brood should not surpass hers. If Maria's son Prince [Kitty's most beloved slave] cut down wood with more dexterity and dispatch than any one in the province, the mighty Caesar, son of Diana, cut down wheat and threshed it better than he" (Humphreys 37). As she goes on to tell, their sisters were accomplished as well: "His sister Betty, who to her misfortune was a beauty of her kind, and possessed with equal to her beauty, was the best seamstress and laundress I have known, and plain, unpretending Rachel, sister to Prince, wife to Tytus alias Tyte and head cook, dressed dinners that might have pleased Apicus" (Humphreys 37-38). They were allowed pets and gardens, while they excelled in all types of skills and also defended the family.

Both Eliza and Alexander, staying with the Schuylers for prolonged periods "would have seen their own future wealth, via inheritance, tied up at least partially in slave property. And they would have been concerned about what offering freedom to enslaved people would have meant for the maintenance of their lives" (Harris 82). Emancipation would have meant a loss of labor and a smaller inheritance in future, from a family whose fortune was built on slave labor. The practice continued through their lives, offering a moral quandary in the fight for independence.

THE SCHUYLER SISTERS

"Me? I loved him" all three sisters announce in the introductory number. The use of "I" not "we" makes this personal—each loved him in a different way. Since young Peggy later plays Maria, she brings in the forbidden affair as well as the innocent love of the sister-in-law. Of course, beside Angelica's love of the mind, Eliza is also all-encompassing and epic as Hamilton's heart.

"Eliza was the classic middle sister and the peacemaker. She took after her father, with a strong-boned face a bit too thin and angular to be called beautiful on a young woman. She had an enviable figure and a healthy, athletic build from hopping over fences and riding horses fast. But she also had a stubborn independence and a native modesty that made it easy to overlook her amid her flashier sisters" (Mazzeo 25). Angelica was the socialite, and Peggy could be more than a little rebellious. Caught between them, Eliza was a quiet, soothing presence who kept the three sisters together.

Angelica (Engeltke in Dutch) was the oldest by eighteen months, with Peggy thirteen months younger than Eliza. There were three younger brothers: John, Philip Jr., and Rensselaer. However, there was a seven-year gap between John and Peggy, leaving the three older sisters very much as a trio. Eventually, little sisters Cordelia and Catherine joined the lineup. Their fates were all quite lively.

> Their eldest little brother and heir to. the largest share of the family's fortune, John Schuyler, dutifully married the patroon's nineteen-year-old sister, Elizabeth Van Rensselaer, in a grand society wedding. The next two boys, Eliza's brothers Philip and Rensselaer, however, exasperated their father. Rensselaer was ungovernable and had been since he was seven. Eliza's brother Philip Jr. was either too busy partying or too dull to pass his college courses at Columbia—nobody quite knew which was the problem. He was the only one of the Schuyler boys to go to college, and his father was determined to see through the investment. But it had not turned out with the boys as General Schuyler expected. Eliza's father candidly confessed to Angelica that her brother Philip Jr., was a disappointment, and Angelica sympathized with her father's concerns about gambling especially... Just when General Schuyler's patience was completely exhausted, young Philip Schuyler made another rash decision and ran off to marry a local eighteen-year-old beauty and heiress. (Mazzeo 124)

Young Cornelia, meanwhile, fell in love with Washington Morton and brought him home to meet her parents. They disliked him, considering him too young and unfocused, and her father insisted she break off all contact. She refused and soon ran off with him. As Washington bragged later to his family, "I got my wife in opposition to them both. She leapt from a Two Story Window into my arms and abandoning every thing for me gave the most convincing proof of what a husband most Desire to Know that his wife Loves him" (Mazzeo 200). Kitty and Philip Schuyler were worried for their daughter, and Philip Schuyler confided to Eliza that he wished Cornelia happy, "if she can possibly enjoy it, with a man of such an untoward disposition as her husband—I ap-

HAMILTON'S WOMEN

prehend very much that he will render her miserable, and increase my affection." They visited Cornelia's parents at Albany, but things went badly. "His conduct, whilst here has been as usual, most preposterous," Philip Schuyler reported. "Seldom an evening at home, and seldom even at dinner—I have not thought it prudent to say the least word to him ... as advice on such an irregular character is thrown away." (Mazzeo 200). As Mazzeo reports, "Sadly, her father's predictions were not unjust. Cornelia had years to regret her youthful impulse, and the marriage was rocky from the beginning" (200).

All this occurred far after the show, of course. When Hamilton and Eliza were courting, only the three oldest girls were out in society. Angelica was the most sophisticated and socially ambitious of the three sisters, a lover of romances in novels and poetry as well as real life. "'A very Pretty Young Lady,' as one visitor noted emphatically, she looked the most like their mother, who had been a beauty" (Mazzeo 25). She was also quite a flirt. Speaking fluent French, she charmed important, clever men like Thomas Jefferson and Benjamin Franklin with her long, clever letters.

Angelica essentially grew up in New York City when her father had served in the colony assembly. There, she would have attended parties and made aristocratic visits, event while listening to impassioned speeches at the Liberty Pole on the Common. When George Washington had been made supreme commander of the army, she would have watched his parade, with her own father riding beside him. Sometimes her younger sisters were there too. In this, their first number "The Schuyler Sisters" takes root.

> But perhaps one of the most incredible aspects of *Hamilton* and its ladies is that not only are these women strong and smart as individuals, they are wildly supportive of one another. "We are so in love with each other and we feel so powerful when we're all together," Goldsberry says of her fellow Schuyler sisters. It's a bond that translated so well behind the scenes, that it influenced the award-winning show itself. In fact, Cephas Jones shares with Smart Girls that, "[Renee, Phillipa, and I] had such a tight bond and we were singing all together constantly. [*Hamilton* creator

VALERIE ESTELLE FRANKEL

> and star] Lin-Manuel Miranda actually rewrote [the song] 'The Schuyler Sisters' and put more harmonies in and made it more who we are when we're together." (Semigran)

Dressed like society women in bustles but singing like a Destiny's Child R. & B. girl group, Angelica and her sisters quote the newly written Declaration of Independence—"We hold these truths to be self-evident, that all men are created equal"—then Angelica raps: "And when I meet Thomas Jefferson …I'm a compel him to include women in the sequel!" Clearly, "The first time you meet these women [in the show], they are coming out and saying what they want and what they deserve and standing for what they believe in," says Cephas Jones, who pulls double duty as Peggy and Maria in the original production (Semigran). Goldsberry—who portrays Angelica Schuyler—perhaps puts it best when it comes to playing a woman from *any* time period: "We know no matter what situation a woman is in, she is hugely influencing everything that's around her. There's no box that you can put a woman in" (Semigran).

> Peggy, Angelica and Eliza enter New York in peach, yellow, and seafoam Colonial dresses. Angelica's dress is the most elaborate and Peggy's is the simplest, reflecting their personalities and roles in the story. Eliza's soft green shows her as a nurturer happy to tend her garden. (Also, as Hamilton dons green to deal with politics and money, they become a matched set as perfect couple.) Peggy's yellow is youthful, innocent, untried. Eliza's peach is more sensual. Each also has a musical motif attached to her name, repeated whenever the name is used. (Frankel)

The sisters enter the show with their "I want" song, a staple of musical theater that provide the audience with a glimpse of a character's inner desires. The song is also a love letter to New York, emphasizing the bustle and transformation of the "greatest city in the world," on the cusp of Revolution. Still, their need for "a mind [presumably a male one like Hamilton's] at work" suggests how much their triple story will be tied to Hamilton's in this adaptation.

Many critics see Angelica's introduction as fitting for Hamilton's equal: "While Hamilton passionately raps about his vision for a free nation, Angelica leads her two sisters Eliza and Peggy in their introductory number 'The Schuyler Sisters' with equal, if not more, verve and vigor....It's a girl-powered moment that solicits many a snap and woot in agreement, and rightfully so," Sarah Halle Corey explains in "The Women of *Hamilton* Are Your New Feminist Sheroes." Alison Dobrick, in her essay in *Hamilton and Philosophy: Revolutionary Thinking,* adds, "Renee Goldsberry's distinct delivery of the word 'women' excludes how she feels about the first Declaration mentioning only men's rights. She plans to compel, not to mildly suggest" (183). Of course, Angelica's sassy demand does not actually come to fruition: "It's exciting to hear the Schuyler sisters demand political equality, but the show continues on past this song to depict the men who actually got to build the American government. One can't help but remember that those sisters actually wouldn't get to see women's suffrage in their lifetimes," Corey sadly concludes.

The love triangle between Eliza and Angelica is interesting, as both are presented sympathetically, in a departure from musical theater norms. More often, there is a sweet, feminine good girl versus a rebel—one cast as good and the other as fundamentally flawed:

> In *Les Misérables,* Cosette is obedient and passive, while Eponine brawls with her father in the streets. In the film version of *The Sound of Music,* the immaculately coiffed Baroness watches in horror as Maria exuberantly overturns a rowboat in her homemade dress. *Jekyll and Hyde's* Emma is chaste and pure, while Lucy is a prostitute who tells her customers to "bring on the men." And traditionally, musicals are not shy or subtle about telling their audiences which of the two women is worth rooting for. Sometimes the bad woman turns out to be secretly cold, like the Baroness with her villainous plan to send the von Trapp children to boarding school ("Baroness Machiavelli!" another character exclaims)...The problem with this narrative structure is that it asks the audience to sort all women into two types and then pick one of those types to hate: This kind of woman is okay, but not this kind. It suggests there are two ways to be a woman, one of which is acceptable and one of which is despicable. (Grady)

VALERIE ESTELLE FRANKEL

Hamilton avoids this by lauding both women—one Hamilton's great love and the other his intellectual peer. Further, the musical allows him to love both in a relationship that prizes mutual support, not jealousy.

In the expressive fandom outside the show, the women continue to inspire feminism through their attitudes, even in a plot mostly focused on the men. L. M. Elliott explains in an essay on the historical sisters:

> One of the myriad things Lin-Manuel Miranda does so beautifully in *Hamilton: An American Musical* is his portrayal of the profound symbiosis among the Schuyler Sisters: Angelica, Eliza, AND Peggy. The sisterhood has captivated women across America. With a kind of defiant delight, fans quote Miranda's wonderfully proto-feminist lyrics: "I want a revelation," and "include women in the sequel." Teens strike the sassy peace-sign/snap pose of the trio's reprisal: "Work!" With this as their pop culture vernacular, Miranda may well be responsible for a whole generation of young women now determined to "be part of the (national) narrative."

Further, the actresses continued making history when they sang at the Super Bowl and casually added "and sisterhood" to "America the Beautiful." With this they emphasize women's influence on history. "It makes even more sense when you talk to each of these women independently. Soo, Goldsberry, and Cephas Jones all credited their mothers as the most influential woman in their lives, and they all are humbled by the impact the show has had on the masses. Most notably, they all have similar advice for young women pursuing their dreams, whether it's hitting the Great White Way or going their own way: be yourself, in every sense of the word" (Semigran). After the show, the actresses found different paths, but each continued speaking out for empowerment.

ANGELICA'S MARRIAGE

Angelica's original actress Renée Elise Goldsberry was a veteran of television, appearing on *Ally McBeal, One Life to Give,* and *The Good Wife.* She moved to Broadway to play Nala in *The Lion King* and then Mimi during the last few months of *Rent* in 2008. In Hamilton's early stages, she was brought onboard. Of course, this part helped her break out as a star. In 2017, Goldsberry starred as Henrietta Lacks in the HBO television film *The Immortal Life of Henrietta Lacks.* In 2018, she appeared in the Netflix science fiction series *Altered Carbon.* For her work in the production, she won a 2015 Drama Desk Award, the Lucille Lortel Award for Outstanding Featured Actress in a Musical, and the 2016 Tony Award for Best Featured Actress in a Musical. In addition, she shared in the 2016 Grammy for Best Musical Theater Album.

Goldsberry has also performed with co-stars Miranda and Daveed Diggs on the BET cypher, rapping about famous women in history like Sojourner Truth and Rosa Parks. "It's very much in line with what our show does and what women rappers do," Goldsberry said. "They're all very powerful—you have to be powerful to be a rapper. It seemed like a very natural fit, especially when our show is celebrating history to focus on powerful women" (Purcell). Her vivaciousness and speedy rap helped define Angelica's role in the show.

The character's rap in her first central song "Satisfied" is significant, emphasizing that she operates on the men's level with incredible intelligence. "If a song is written well, you know what you have to say," Goldsberry says. "Even in this instance, this woman is talking very fast, and making decisions in an instant, but she is extremely analytical. The path is very clear. The path is so intrinsic" (Miranda 79). "Renee was the first one who came in and made us say, 'Oh, she thinks exactly that fast'" Miranda recalls. "She's demonstrating that Angelica read Hamilton the moment she saw him, but it didn't stop her from falling in love with him, and didn't stop her calculating *in a moment* to yield to her sister's love for him" (Miranda 79).

Onstage, she's the one female who raps, with the rapidity displaying the speed of Angelica's thoughts but also the actress's talent. In this scene, just by her music, she breaks conventions. Miranda tweeted, "I want to fast forward to when high schools do Hamilton & the girl playing Angelica Scuyler gets to spit *the hardest bars in the show*" (79). Goldsberry also challenges the idea of what one is "supposed" to be: "As women, we put a lot of pressure on ourselves to be perfect — I know I do—and live up to this idea of what women are supposed to be. The one thing that is certain: is it's not possible to do that at all times. Every day we have to define what being a woman means, and it's going to be different from the day before," she explains (Semigran).

In history, Angelica was already married during Hamilton and Eliza's courtship. The show's change gives Angelica and Hamilton dramatic tension but also, in a feminist flip, makes it her choice whether to pursue him or decide against it and present him to her sister. More rebellious than Eliza, the actual Angelica eloped. While the show doesn't emphasize this point, it's striking that Eliza anxiously waits for her father to give permission or not, while Angelica gives no mention of her family approving or disapproving her match. In "Satisfied," she describes her duty to the family to marry well, but this is a personal choice she is making through her practicality, unlike smitten Eliza who cares nothing for Hamilton's background. In "Nonstop," Angelica frankly owns up to marrying someone "who always pays" and "is not a lot of fun," emphasizing that she has chosen money over love. Of course, in the context of the time, as Angelica explains in "Satisfied," this is the one choice she has, and her lack of family mentioned influencing her choice in "Nonstop" emphasizes that she's made it for herself, in a moment of strength and agency.

HAMILTON'S WOMEN

"Her portrait reveals a dramatically different personality from shy, submissive Betsey. Angelica had an angular face with mocking dark eyes and a sensuous mouth that seems poised to make a witty-or a seductive-quip. Sophistication, worldliness, and even a certain recklessness emanate from Angelica," Fleming tells (225). On Angelica's first grown-up visit to New York City, she was struck by the romance of the governor's daughter climbing the garden wall to run off with a young captain in a great social scandal. "Her impulsive actions would forever defined Angelica's idea of the romantic" (Mazzeo 18). She came back to her family far more elegant and adult. Eliza joked with her friend decades later over "Angelica's early air of Elegance and dignity when she first returned from New York" (Mazzeo 19). Both girls went off to boarding school in New York to learn more social graces.

When John Carter, a young Revolutionary officer with a British origin, came calling in 1776, he was mysterious enough that Angelica was smitten. Her father feared he was a spy and ordered his daughter to break off contact, but that only made Angelica more eager. In June 1777, she ran away with him. They reached her grandfather's house, and the scandalized man had no choice but to see the couple wed as Angelica had compromised herself. He also extracted more of the young man's story—his real name was John Church, a gentleman from London, who had run away from his apprenticeship to a merchant there, fallen in with wild young men, taken to gambling, and finally stolen from his uncle to settle his debts. Cut off by his uncle and also guilty of dueling, he had fled to America and joined the rebels, as the British would have discovered his unsavory background.

Carter, born into the British aristocracy, seemed showy and frivolous to the patriots. A war profiteer, he felt less committed than they were. In fact, Chernow observes that Church amassed "fantastic wealth" during the Revolution selling supplies to the French and American forces (134). His European sophistication must have been compelling for Angelica, as she and her sisters were banished to Albany and barred from the enemy-occupied New York City. Schuyler meanwhile kept him around, hoping he might help gather intelligence among the loyalists.

Angelica's choice in husband is perplexing, frankly. In 1777, when her father was General of the Northern Army and desperately trying to counter a British invasion from Canada, Angelica eloped with a man who'd been sent by Congress to check her father's accounts, accusing Schuyler of poor command. Needless to say, Schuyler didn't much like the guy. Her suitor was also cloaked in mystery, having recently fled England, either to escape gambling debts or retribution for a duel, and adopted an alias, John Carter. It's unclear whether the Schuylers knew this. In any case, Carter's hasty emigration doesn't come across as sincere revolutionary fervor promising Thomas Paine style "revelation." Eventually, Carter did play an important role in the Revolution, as commissary for the French Army. But he also amassed a fortune doing so. As such Carter would be a controversial patriot at best. So why him? Angelica's father "was loaded," one of the richest and most influential men in upstate New York, so there was no need for his firstborn "to social climb" or "to marry rich" for the family's sake. And in 1777, Carter didn't offer any of that. (Elliott)

Stuck in Albany, away from the sophistication of New York, Angelica appears to have been bored enough to be beguiled by a handsome face. She was willful and romantic too. "So while Miranda may have changed the specifics of her early life to fit his musical's time-constraints, he completely captures the yearning intellectual and scintillating conversationalist Angelica was and the quick, deep affinity she felt for Hamilton. Miranda's presentation of the fierce loyalty among the Schuyler sisters, no matter what wedge a man might drive between them, is also spot-on" (Elliott).

Angelica's father was furious and cut her off. General Schuyler writes to his friend William Duer, the man who had introduced John to the family: "Carter and my eldest daughter ran off and were married on the twenty-third of July. Unacquainted with his family connections and situation in life the matter was extremely disagreeable and I signified it to them" (Humphreys 191). However, John Carter didn't have the money to support a wealthy wife, and had counted on a

HAMILTON'S WOMEN

settlement from the family. At last, Philip Schuyler relented and allowed the young couple to move in—partially because they were destitute, and partially to end all the gossip and feuding. As Philip Schuyler went on in his letter, "as there is no undoing this Gordian Knot... I frowned, I made them humble themselves, forgave, and called them home" (Mazzeo 47). Mazzeo describes their relationship afterward:

> The chilly reception and the groveling apologies Angelica's father demanded of the couple should have been a hint to John and Angelica not to inflame the situation. It was certainly enough to persuade Eliza that she would never marry except with her papa's permission. Neither John nor Angelica, however, ever showed much sense in matters of finances or diplomacy. John, who took a liberal view of his right to the money of other people, considered that he was entitled to a share of the family fortune as a marriage portion. He was a man who took what he wanted from life without so much as a by-your-leave and thought it enough afterward to smooth any ruffled -feathers with a gallant thank-you. That others saw this as underhanded and manipulative he could never fathom. His young wife, on the other hand, was simply spoiled. It had never occurred to Angelica that she would need to think about money. Papa had always paid for everything. (47)

Living with the family, John took advantage, ordering expensive goods and charging them to his still-angry father-in-law. After a time, John resigned his commission and he and Angelica moved to Boston. There, he fussed about the fancy food they had trouble procuring and fanciful Angelica struggled to keep a budget while Eliza stayed with them to help with this and with Angelica's pregnancy. The couple's first children were named Philip and Kitty to make amends to Angelica's parents. In the evenings there were balls. "The idea of the flirtatious Angelica acting as the chaperone to her younger, steadier sister raised more than one astonished eyebrow. Angelica was known, especially, for her risqué fashion choices, and people tutted that it was the young Mrs. Carter who needed a chaperone (Mazzeo 60). Next, Eliza visited her aunt and uncle, falling for Hamilton on the trip, and she married properly at her parents' home.

VALERIE ESTELLE FRANKEL

On July 27, 1783, John, Angelica, and their small children, Philip, Kitty, and John, set sail for Paris. "John was now a vastly wealthy man. The account books for him showed that he and his partner, Jeremiah Wadsworth, had-raked in profits of nearly 35,000 pounds—earnings upwards of a modern equivalent of $46 million. The partners were owed more payments from the French government for unpaid wartime bills, and they were traveling to France to collect" (Mazzeo 113). He also wanted to clear his debts and show off his success in his home country. They lived there for sixteen years, with a few visits to America. However, Angelica worried over her husband's staggering bets at the horse races and frantic social scene, as she confided to Hamilton. His "head is full of politics, he is so desirous of making one in the British House of Commons," in her words that Angelica hardly saw him (Mazzeo 124).

"Angelica's husband bought a palatial country estate near London and became part of the circle around the Prince of Wales, a social whirl in which the men gambled themselves into near bankruptcy and drank themselves into insensibility and the idea of marital fidelity drew guffaws. Almost everyone imitated the prince and had a mistress" (Fleming 225). He also became a member of Parliament. It's unclear whether her husband cheated, but as early as 1785, Angelica was telling Hamilton that "he no longer hears me." (Fleming 225). She often felt lonely despite the glamor and complained of a society "confined to chill, gloomy Englishmen" (Chernow 282). She wrote to Eliza of seeing the royal family at the theater but to her, "What are Kings and Queens to an American who has seen a Washington!" (Chernow 282).

The pair had eight children, five girls and three boys. Philip Schuyler Church (1778–1861) served as a U.S. Army captain and aide de camp to Alexander Hamilton in 1798–1800, during the Quasi-War with France. He married Ann Stuart, daughter of General Walter Stuart. "The President gave the bride away and presented her with his miniature surrounded by diamonds" (Humphreys 238). He also founded the town

30

HAMILTON'S WOMEN

of Angelica, New York, named for his mother. Further, he was the second in the duel that killed his cousin, Philip Hamilton. The other children were Kitty (1779–1839), John Barker (1781–1865), Elizabeth Matilda (1783–1867), Richard Hamilton Church (1785–1786), Alexander (1792–1803), Richard Stephen (1798–1889), and Angelica (b. 1800).

In Paris, painter John Trumbull (referenced in a cut musical song about the quarreling statesmen and also one of Angelica's portrait artists) introduced Thomas Jefferson to Maria Cosway. She was a married painter, and he adored her on sight and wrote her famous love letters. They enjoyed opera and theater and music together, and the lady hosted artistic salons. These Angelica attended as Maria's special friend. "If I did not love her so much, I should fear her rivalship," Maria wrote to Jefferson (Adams 240).

Thomas Jefferson, now the U.S. ambassador to France, was smitten with Angelica. She had asked Trumbull for a copy of the miniature of Jefferson he had painted, and Jefferson wrote to her, "The memorial of me which you have from Trumbull is the most worthless part of me. Could he paint my friendship to you, it would be something out of the common line" (Adams 241). He wrote to her after she departed, "The morning you left us, all was wrong, even the sunshine was provoking, with which I never quarreled before," he wrote her. "I took it into my head he shone only to throw light on our loss: to present a cheerfulness not at all in unison with my mind. I mounted my horse earlier than common. I took by instinct the road you had taken" (Baskervill). "I think I have discovered a method of preventing this dejection of mind on any future parting," he wrote her on Feb. 17, the same day she left Paris to return to London. "It is this," he explained. "When you come again I will employ myself solely in finding or fancying that you have some faults. & I will draw a veil over all your good qualities, if I can find one large enough." He also taunted Maria Cosway in his letters that he might travel with Angelica (Adams 237).

"There is something going on, some sort of attraction"

between Jefferson and Angelica, says Jan Lewis, professor of history at Rutgers University and author of *The Pursuit of Happiness: Family and Values in Jefferson's Virginia*. Six months after they met, Jefferson seductively proposes that she accompany him on a vacation to America. "Think of it, my friend, and let us begin a negotiation on the subject. You shall find in me all the spirit of accommodation with which Yoric began his with the fair Piedmontese." This references a scene in the popular Laurence Sterne novel *Sentimental Journey*, in which these characters are forced to share a room at a crowded Italian country inn and eventually have sex. Though their flirtations may have been confined to letters, Jefferson and Angelica were apparently quite suggestive. While this might have added an interesting leg to the love triangle on the show, Angelica does not encounter Jefferson there, or even offer the personal advice on him that she did in history. Miranda reveals that he couldn't find a way to fit Angelica's relationship with Jefferson into the story, though he included it in his guide *Hamilton: The Revolution* (44). Once again, interesting possibilities for her role are curtailed.

As time went on, Angelica's daughter Kitty was a playmate of Jefferson's daughter, Mary ("Polly") Jefferson. These social connections made Angelica instrumental in the release of Lafayette from the prison at Olmutz, Austria. Once again, she affected history, doing what Hamilton, in his second cabinet battle, could not, though this mark on history goes unmentioned.

Other men admired her too, like the Marquis de Lafayette. Louisa Adams wondered at her relationship with the ambassador to Britain, Thomas Pickney, as he visited her house quite often and sometimes left very late. Her social circle included the Prince of Wales (later King George IV), Whig party leader Charles James Fox, and playwright Richard Brinsley Sheridan. She was a glittering fixture in Europe, charming its great leaders even as her husband stumbled to achieve their good graces.

HAMILTON'S WOMEN

ANGELICA AND
HAMILTON

She had charmed bluebloods in Paris and London and New York. Gouverneur Morris, Gotham's best-known rake, had been so dazzled that he claimed Angelica could have whatever part of his body she preferred. But there seemed to be only one man who aroused this temptress>s deepest feelings. It was not her fat, stolid, monosyllabic British husband, who had made a fortune during the Revolution supplying the American and French armies. The man was her brother-in-law, Alexander Hamilton. (Fleming 225)

A fully formed character and foil for the gentler Eliza, the musical's Angelica gets to grow, change and suffer, as emphasized in "Satisfied," which shows the crack in the perfect mask she presents in "Helpless." These parallel songs show Angelica meeting Hamilton, first from her sister's point of view, and then from her own. As the show rewinds to the meeting at the ball, her memories are lit in the blue of memory instead of Eliza's dreamy pink.

The "rewind" effect and paralleling of the two courtship scenes in which one sister then the other recalls meeting Hamilton offer a fascinating twist. "As a student of history, Miranda carefully weaves the two numbers to show the uncertainty each of the three experienced at that moment, and to introduce the importance of understanding each narrator's distinct perspective" (Adelman 291). Who tells the story truly becomes paramount. Adelman continues: "By presenting the two perspectives back to back, with the same setup and much of the same dialogue, Miranda makes clear that the story looks different depending on your perspective. In a world where many people believe there is one true story and a plethora of 'biased' accounts, placing two descriptions of the same event on equal footing is not only educational, but also a bit subversive" (292). Miranda is offering advice on how to engage with history even as he reimagines it. "For him, 'history' is about possible pathways, choices, and contingency. It is

33

also, crucially, about interpreting the past through the lens of the present" (Adelman 292).

As she reveals, meeting Alexander has truly affected her: "I remember that night I just might regret that night for the rest of my days," she explains. "I have never been the same...You set my heart aflame, every part aflame, this is not a game." In fact, she is so intelligent that she has the monologue of "Satisfied" with herself—she has no confidante.

Miranda notes that "Satisfied," like "Helpless," has multiple meanings. "There is all manner of satisfaction—sexual, emotional, financial. It's also a code word used in dueling—'to demand satisfaction' It's also onomatopoeic—it feels like it sounds, satisfying to sing. We wring every last bit from it" (Miranda 80). Aside from a sexual meaning, which Angelica responds to coldly as a woman of the time was supposed to, Hamilton's flirtation with her emphasizes their parallel ambition, as the first line literally addresses having enough—having so much that they will stop striving, something neither one has ever had:

> Hamilton: You strike me as a woman who has never been satisfied.
> Angelica: I'm sure I don't know what you mean you forget yourself.
> Hamilton: You're like me, I'm never satisfied.

If Eliza was "Helpless" Angelica wants to be "Satisfied"—on Twitter, Miranda quoted the real letter from Angelica to Hamilton that inspired the song's lyrics: "You are happy my dear friend to find consolation in 'words & thoughts.' I cannot be so easily satisfied" (Eggert). As he adds: "The lyrics to 'Satisfied'—in which Angelica Schuyler recounts how Hamilton and her sister Eliza met and married—are some of the most intricate I've ever written. I can't even rap them, but Renee Elise Goldsberry, who plays Angelica—that's her conversational speed. That's how fast she thinks" (DiGiacomo).

Goldsberry describes Angelica as a "foremother of America" and says, "I really think if she were a man, she would have been president" (Purcell). She's politically astute and advises Hamilton, on the show and in history. Of course,

HAMILTON'S WOMEN

while their minds are similar (as shown by her furiously fast rap), their opportunities are very different. Chad William Timm explains in his essay on legacy, "History Has Its Eyes on You" that women's roles at the time were strikingly confined: "While Alexander can use his intelligence and motivation to aspire to great political influence Angelica is forced to use her intelligence and motivation to marry a politically influential man. *Hamilton* points out this contradiction and reminds us of the injustices experienced by women while showing us their resilience in the face of inequality" (202-203). Of course, the show acknowledges this inequality, as well as Angelica's awareness of it.

> *Hamilton* recognizes that in the 18th century, both rebellious and conventionally feminine women are trapped. Angelica has the intellect and the drive to make valuable contributions to the emerging republic, but instead she is stuck behind the scenes, "a girl in a world in which / my only job is to marry rich." Her refrain throughout the show is, "I will never be satisfied," because it is her tragedy to live in a world where she cannot do the kind of work that would satisfy her. In contrast, Eliza has the opportunity and means to do the kind of domestic work that she loves and is good at, but she lives in a world where this kind of work is not valued, because it's considered less important than the political work Hamilton does. Eliza is stuck at the fringes of history, whispering, "Oh, let me be a part of the narrative," and her refrain is, "That would be enough," because it is her tragedy to live in a world where she is denied the little respect she asks for. (Grady)

In history, she had brothers but also chose her own marriage and lifestyle. Miranda confesses, "Okay, so Philip Schuyler really had *loads* of sons. I conveniently forgot that while I was writing this in service of a larger point: Angelica is a world class intellect in a world that does not allow her to flex it" (80). Angelica's dreams for political advancement are like Alexander's, though she can only achieve them by marrying well. Angelica spells this out in the song, showing that, just as Alexander chooses promotions and fame over his wife (or at least takes her for granted) in "That Would be Enough" and "Hurricane," Angelica makes a similar choice here. She can have love or wealth, class and power, and chooses ac-

35

VALERIE ESTELLE FRANKEL

cordingly. She even reflects that "He's after me cause I'm a Schuyler sister that elevates the status/I'd have to be naive to set that aside." She wants to marry better, but knows Eliza, the second daughter, will settle for less and be content (though ironically Eliza became more famous in history through her marriage to one of the Founding Fathers). Dobrick adds:

> Hamilton takes place, in the words of Angelica Schuyler, "in a time in which my only job is to marry rich." Howard Zinn evocatively termed women of the Revolutionary era "the intimately oppressed": living intimately alongside men, but unable to own property or vote, or even engage freely in public or private life. Strictly defined roles as daughters, wives, and mothers dominate the Schuyler sisters' and most other women's lives. Hamilton radiantly depicts female characters who, though legally "helpless" on their own, show more intelligence and accomplish more legacy building on behalf of men than many of the men who work on their legacy full time. (179-180)

This choice explores feminism *within the context of the time*—Angelica selects her own husband, one who will give her the life she prefers. Since she cannot go to war or join Washington's cabinet, this is her best option. "Angelica is *as* driven, intelligent, and aspirational as Alexander Hamilton but lacks the freedom to choose," Timm adds (202). It's also mentioned that her great intellect is what blocks her from happiness (a similar obstacle to Hamilton's own fatal flaw). She explains that she might have wed him "If I hadn't sized him up so quickly," if she hadn't reflected on all the issues of class and duty keeping them apart. She ends her song with "I will never be satisfied," a final parallel with ambitious Hamilton.

This compelling twist—that Angelica wanted Hamilton but passed him over for her own future and her sister's, has a lasting effect on the rest of all three's relationship through the show: "When we first see the Schuyler sisters interact with the men of the story, it seems as if we might be witnessing a classic love triangle, with both Angelica and Eliza pining after Hamilton. Yet, Angelica chooses not to pursue a man, acting

HAMILTON'S WOMEN

in favor of both her sister and the greater good of her country," Corey decides. It's a small action but a decidedly feminist one.

This is her role in the play, to be Hamilton's confidante and emotional affair—the one he neglects Eliza to pour his heart out to. The show suggests that Angelica, as well as being witty and flirtatious, can understand the politics involved and give better advice while Eliza only listens supportively. While this isn't particularly touched on in the show, Angelica had tidbits of gossip to share about Jefferson—particularly his indiscretion with Sally Hemings. On the show, however, any impact she has on history is blunted. This is a disappointing turn for the character.

> Angelica becomes Hamilton's soulmate and though her first song suggests she'll be an active participant in the country's formation, she does nothing but pine for Alexander after arranging the match between him and her beautiful and vacuous sister, Eliza. At one point, she urges him to negotiate with Jefferson, again hinting at her backstage power to influence politics. In spite of Goldsberry's extraordinary performance, Angelica simply doesn't have much to do in the musical. In the end, she plays the role of the muse, the supportive sister, the intellectual equal of Hamilton who plays no overt role in the country's formation. In other words, she is introduced as a remarkable, powerful and potentially ground-breaking character but ultimately occupies a familiar gender stereotype. (Wolf)

Though she's striking and formidable, the show gives her little of import to do—either to shape Hamilton or history.

Angelica adds to her sister later, "I'm just sayin', if you really loved me, you would share him" (a historical quip in her letters that graces the musical's love triangle). This suggestion is provocative, rule-breaking and funny like Angelica herself, but also foreshadows the messy relationship's future. Chernow adds, likely fueling this plot on the show, "It is hard to escape the impression that Hamilton's married life was sometimes a curious *menage a trois* with two sisters who were only a year apart. Angelica must have sensed that her incessant adoration of Hamilton, far from annoying or threatening her beloved younger sister, filled her with ecstatic pride. Their shared love for Hamilton seemed to deepen their sisterly bond" (134). Chernow continues:

> Starting with that first winter in Morristown, Hamilton was drawn almost magnetically to Eliza's married older sister Angelica, and spent the rest of his life beguiled by both Eliza and Angelica, calling them 'my dear brunettes' Together the two eldest sisters formed a composite portrait of Hamilton's ideal woman, each appealing to a different facet of his personality. Eliza reflected Hamilton's earnest sense of purpose., determination, and moral rectitude while Angelica exhibited his worldly side—the wit, charm, and vivacity that so delighted people in social intercourse. (133).

This moment establishes the relationship in the show—Angelica will always be the clever, flirtatious one, but her standing aside for her sister is a real, permanent decision that shapes the future of the nation. If Angelica had not been married in real life, it's quite possible that she and Hamilton would have chosen each other. Chernow notes, "It seems plausible that Hamilton would have proposed to Angelica not Eliza if the older sister had been eligible" (133).

THE LOVE TRIANGLE

Angelica historically was just such a flirt as in the paired songs, both in America and later in Europe: "Angelica had a more mysterious femininity than her sister, the kind that often exerts a powerful hold on the male imagination. A playful seductress, she loved to engage in repartee, discuss books, strum the guitar, and talk about current affairs" (Chernow 133).

By contrast, Eliza's letters lacked sophistication and Hamilton often chided her for not writing enough. "Angelica's letters, on the other hand, went toe-to-toe with Hamilton's in philosophy and clever flirtatiousness," Elliot notes. There was also an obvious admiration for her brother-in-law. In 1784, writing to her sister from Europe, she mentioned Hamilton's

HAMILTON'S WOMEN

name fourteen times in a single letter. In another, she requested newspapers, especially "those that contain your husband's writings" (Fleming 225). She ordered Eliza to tell Hamilton how much "I envy you the fame of so clever a husband, one who writes so well; God bless him and may he long continue to be the friend and brother of your affectionate ... Angelica" (Fleming 225). Chernow writes that "the attraction between Hamilton and Angelica was so potent and obvious that many people assumed they were lovers. At the very least, theirs was a friendship of unusual ardor" (186).

Renée Elise Goldsberry adds, "It feels wrong but it's also necessary and crucial for her existence. He gives her something that she gets nowhere else, and she has to have it." At the same time, both are devoted to Eliza. "The love affair is really Eliza and loving him through her" Goldsberry concludes (Miranda 167).

As Elliot adds, 'The comma-play, for instance, that Miranda presents in 'Take a Break,' (which he has jokingly called 'comma sexting') was actually an implied endearment penned by Angelica, known admiringly by her contemporaries as 'the thief of hearts'." By 1787, Angelica was writing playfully endearing letters to Hamilton "Indeed my dear, Sir," she wrote, playing games with the comma placement. Hamilton was incredibly busy composing The Federalist Papers, to persuade thousands of voters to support the new constitution. However, he was struck by Angelica's comma: "There was a most critical comma in your last letter. It is in my interest that it should have been designed; but I presume it was accidental." He added that he had a high opinion of her "discernment" (a word he underlined) so he hoped that she would read his reply in a certain mood that would enable her to "divine that in which I write it." Angelica had in fact thanked him for strewing so many "roses" (compliments) in her path in a previous letter. In his, Hamilton told her that these pretty phrases had become "only a feeble image" of what he now wanted to convey to her. He then closed these loving phrases with a misplaced comma of his own: "Adieu, *ma chere, soeur.* A. Hamilton" (my dear, sister) (Fleming 226)

By contrast, as Chernow notes, "Church's letters present a cold businessman, devoid of warmth or humor. Very involved in politics, he could be tactless in expressing his opinions...He lacked the intellectual breadth and civic commitment that made Hamilton so compelling to Angelica. On the other hand, he provided Angelica with the opulent, high-society life that she apparently craved" (134). She had successfully married for position indeed.

> Angelica would remain beyond Hamilton's reach in London and Paris for the next six years, the zenith of Hamilton's career. But the intensity of his attraction to her remained a spiritual force in his life, slowly eroding his feelings for Betsey. There was a side of Hamilton's persona that wanted more drama, more ecstasy, than Betsey could inspire with her devotion and fidelity. Sexuality became intermingled with his political triumphs and his growing fame—a phenomenon that would be repeated for more than one American politician in future decades. (Fleming 229)

However, to Eliza's delight, Angelica returned for a visit in 1789 for Washington's inauguration and stayed with them for five months. This, however, provoked far more scandal than flirtatious letters. At one particular ball, one of Angelica's frilly garters fluttered to the dance floor, and down with it came her silk stocking.

> In the 1780s, a lady losing a garter or a bow passed as a chivalric occasion. Peggy—still thought of as "a young wild flirt from Albany, full of glee & apparently desirous of matrimony" in the view of Mr. Otis, despite her marriage to Stephen—plucked her sister's frippery from the floor and put it suggestively in Alexander's buttonhole. To cover their blushes, Alexander hammed up the part of the knight and returned it to Angelica with a flourish, as legend said the gallant King Edward III had once done for his fair mistress. Angelica quipped her thanks and picked up the allusion. She did not know, she retorted gaily, that he had been made royal Knight of the Garter. Such merriment drew unfortunate attention. Peggy, a wit with a raunchy sense of humor, now chimed in acerbically that Alexander would be a Knight of the Bedchamber if he could, and the three rogues all thought it terribly funny. Eliza, long since inured to their tomfoolery, smiled and knew better than to take any of her sisters or her husband

HAMILTON'S WOMEN

> seriously. Those outside their circle, though, saw it differently, especially the wives of Alexander's political enemies. Behind their fans, the sober society ladies pursed their lips and tuttutted. They lived in full view of the public. "I had little of private life in those days," Eliza remembered later. And not everyone who was watching was friendly. (Mazzeo 129-130)

The moment of scandal circulated through New York at the time. Of course, all three were sharing a house during Angelica's visit, in a close scene Angelica alludes to onstage, when she suggests she and Hamilton may have stolen moments at her father's house if Hamilton comes upstate with them. Fleming speculates that an affair was quite possible: "One biographer has found the financial records that Hamilton kept for her in his office ledger very revealing. For an unknown reason, the cash was divided into 'Monies paid to Yourself,' and 'For You.' Certain sums were destined for a 'last' landlady—not the one with whom Angelica stayed and whom John Barker Church paid. Was this 'last' landlady in charge of another set of rooms, where the lovers secretly met?" (Fleming 226).

Angelica was staying with Hamilton and Eliza at the time—until the rumors drove her to a boardinghouse. However, as Hamilton was always working, and she was surrounded by Eliza, her children, and often their parents, there appears to have been little opportunity for an affair, even if there was inclination. "Hamilton's flirtatious correspondence and questionable relationship with Angelica, which some historians and many of Hamilton's political enemies have judged adulterous, did not seem to worry Elizabeth not diminish her strong affection toward her sister—a face which suggests that the relationship between Hamilton and Angelica was likely never more than a flirtation," Villegas concludes (5). The show's relationship between the three—loving, but not beyond the bounds of flirting and wit—appears to have been historically accurate. The two sisters, who helped each other deliver children and wept at partings, appear to have been exceptionally close and thus enjoyed a shared closeness with Eliza's husband.

VALERIE ESTELLE FRANKEL

> But Angelica did wish that she had a husband like Alexander. John was far more imperious, far less tender. He spent weeks in London at his club, carousing with the lads. She had retreated to their country estate near Windsor. Angelica and Alexander's friendship was deep and abiding. There was love and heartfelt care for each other. There was some teasing mixed with flirtation. That was true also. All of it was mixed with a shared sense of the ribald Schuyler family humor. Context is everything. The letters that passed among the three of them—because Eliza was always party to the reading, even if she hated writing—strike the modern eye as clandestine and amorous. To those raised in a culture of sensibility and sentiment, however, they were not proof of anything except deep and intimate affection. (Mazzeo 132)

Eliza appears thoroughly unjealous of the relationship. Chernow reports, "Whatever did—or did not—happen between Alexander and Angelica during her long stay in New York, Eliza was so distraught by her beloved sister's departure that she could not bear to see her off" (282). Hamilton, who did, describes seeing off her ship after the incident, when Angelica's impatient husband ordered her home: "We gazed, we sighed, we wept, and casting 'many a lingering, longing look behind' [a reference to Dido's parting from her own lover]" returned home to give scope to our sorrows, and mingle without restraint our tears and our regrets" (Villegas 88). Continuing to write to her, Hamilton stresses that he always talks about her with his wife, making Angelica a bridge between them: "Betsey and myself make you the last theme of our conversation at night and the first in the morning. We talk of you; we praise you; and we pray for you" (Villegas 89). Chernow points out, "Ironically, Eliza's special attachment to Angelica gave Hamilton a cover for expressing affection for Angelica that would certainly have been forbidden with other women" (134). As his sister, whatever the gossips said, this kind of affection was socially acceptable.

At last, in 1799, Angelica moved back to New York with her husband and children, where they entertained lavishly. Her stylish gowns and heavy jewels evoked old Europe, as did her polished charm. During the scandal of the Reynolds

HAMILTON'S WOMEN

Pamphlet, Angelica was very loyal to Hamilton, publicly and privately. Angelica wrote her sister a long letter describing Hamilton's depression after he had escorted his wife to a ship bound for Albany at her insistence: "You were the subject of his conversation the rest of the evening," she wrote. She begged Eliza to "tranquilize your kind and good heart" and accept her ordeal as almost inevitable for a woman married to a man who achieved fame. If she had married less "near the sun" [an Icarus reference]," Eliza would never have experienced "the pride, the pleasure, the nameless satisfactions" of their relationship (Fleming 242).

On the show, she displays her loyalty to Eliza in a different way, by viciously confronting Hamilton. As with Eliza's burning their love letters, Angelica frames her move to New York as a reaction to the Reynolds Pamphlet instead of part of the normal course of events—something that aids the story arc and raises the drama. It also makes her move an essential part of their tenuous relationship. She ends this sequence by reasserting her commitment to Eliza, insisting, "I will choose her happiness over mine every time," and going off to comfort her instead of Hamilton. As with *Frozen, Supergirl, Marvel's Jessica Jones,* and other films and television of the time, the sister relationship outweighs any romantic interest the heroine may have.

Most of this song, "Congratulations," was cut—unfortunate from the feminist angle as it gave her more of a voice and character arc. In it, she brings her striking quick wit in to summarize exactly how foolish Hamilton has been politically, emphasizing her astuteness: "Congratulations," Angelica's cut song, emphasizes how terrible an idea the Reynold Pamphlet was: "Y'know, you're the only enemy you ever seem to lose to!" Eliza insists they don't need a legacy, but the more politically-minded Angelica shows that Hamilton has permanently tainted his—an accurate observation. In the onstage version, she taunts him with "You could never be satisfied./God, I hope you're satisfied." The word, once used for their flirtation, now slices at him. His lust has destroyed his relationship with Angelica as well as with his wife.

Miranda says, "I love how different it is from everything else in this section. It contributes to the feeling that the world is crashing, pathos within celebration within schadenfreude" (234). Meanwhile, moving from political to personal, Angelica emphasizes her own struggles through a loveless marriage and how important their gentle flirtation has been to her: "I languished in a loveless marriage in London," she tells him. Now she has returned, but as she concludes, "I'm not here for you." She suggests that an affair might have been possible (at least as a distant fantasy), but now that her sister needs her, any chance is over. She and Hamilton don't interact on-screen again, suggesting the death of their flirtation with his deplorable affair.

Through the show and in history, Angelica lives up to her promise and genuinely supports Eliza without ever betraying her. Angelica supports Eliza through her tragedies—her son Philip dies in Angelica's country house and Angelica is there for Hamilton's passing. "One last heartbreaking irony in Hamilton and Angelica's relationship: Carter owned the pistols Hamilton carried to the duel that killed him—the same pair Hamilton's son Philip died holding. Burr and Carter dueled in 1799, but both men survived, leaving the pistols to play their fateful place in history and the musical," Elliott adds.

At age 58, plagued by coughing for years (likely tuberculosis), Angelica died young. Her family fortune was collapsing as well. Eliza stayed with her sister as she slowly succumbed,

> On Sunday, March 13, 1814, Eliza sat with her sister for the last time. In the distance, the church bells of Trinity rang, and in the days to come Eliza would bury another part of her heart there in the graveyard. Angelica was laid into the vault of their Livingston relations, not far from the grave of Alexander. At the funeral, John Church looked beaten, and when Eliza shook his hand goodbye, she guessed that it would be the last time she would see him also; There was nothing to keep John in New York. He set off on the next packet to London, to see what he could salvage of his ruined finances. Eliza never saw him again. John

> Church died abroad in 1818, and if any letters of friendship and grief passed between them; Eliza did not save them. (256-257)

ELIZA'S CHILDHOOD

Eliza Schuyler was born August 9, 1757, into a country torn by the conflicts of the French and Indian War. When she was little, her father inherited two thousand acres in Saratoga, where the Mohawk traditionally hunted. Maintaining treaties with them was foundational in her childhood, while she also learned to sew wampum with the Mohawk girls her age. Later, her distant cousin James Fenimore Cooper immortalized this time in *The Last of the Mohicans*. Eliza and her sisters learned French and English as well as their family's native Flemish and the local Iroquois. There were music and dancing lessons, but also managing the household—something like a large hotel with servants and tenants (and admittedly slaves). As a frontier girl she was an excellent rider and climber. "An athletic woman and a stout walker, she moved with a determined spring in her step. On one picnic excursion, [her admirer Tench] Tilghman watched her laughingly clamber up a steep hillside while less plucky girls required male assistance" (Chernow 130). She accompanied her father to an Iroquois council meeting in place of a son (as her little brothers were too young) and received an Iroquois name that meant "One of Us" (Mazzeo 24).

Before his political career in the new America, Schuyler was a spymaster, directing Canadian, New York and Iroquois spies, intercepting communiques and resealing letters. "Eliza and Angelica would act as his eyes and ears in the Hudson Calley and gather sensitive military intelligence to forward to General Schuyler. They weren't spies exactly. But they weren't not spies either," Mazzeo explains (27). The show fails to mention Eliza and Angelica's contributions to the Revolution (or for that matter, their father's). Instead of revealing them riding like Paul Revere or collecting gossip like Hercules Mulligan, they are only shown slumming in New York City so Burr can flirt with them, and then attending balls where they can have their pick of the officers.

In "The Schuyler Sisters," Eliza is eclipsed by Angelica's assertiveness and appears another debutante, eager to see all the progress. As Wolf notes:

> Eliza, played by the equally fantastic Phillipa Soo, for her part, is seemingly not very bright: in their first number, when they're out in the city and her sister revels the political foment of the time, Eliza sings, "Angelica, remind me what we're looking for..." When she meets Alexander, she's "helpless" with desire, "Down for the count, / And I'm drownin' / in 'em."

While many of her lyrics are a chorus for Angelica, she bursts out with her signature refrain: "Look around, look around at how/ Lucky we are to be alive right now!" While later this will be a point of tension between herself and Hamilton—ambition versus satisfaction—in this scene, she's simply filled with innocent wonder and enjoyment. "Rather than attaching to her name and doing everything she could to vigorously sustain and enhance her ego, Eliza was inspired to subsume her sense of self in a sense of wonder and satisfaction at merely being alive to bear witness and partake of events as they unfolded," Ross notes admiringly (120).

When casting the original show, the team wanted Philippa Soo, who could make Eliza's goodness compelling, as soon as they discovered her in the stage adaptation of *War and Peace: Natasha, Pierre, and the Great Comet of 1812* (Miranda 107). Miranda notes, "Pippa has this sort of elegance and this lit-from-within quality. She's so poised and in such control of what she can do, which is kind of amazing for an actor or actress of her age" (Miranda 107). Throughout the story, she proves a touchstone and support for Hamilton through his tumultuous adventures.

Courting Eliza

"Hamilton may have fancied himself a lady killer, but he might more aptly be characterized as lovelorn and emotionally isolated even amid the social whirl at camp. ...He may have been ambivalent toward marriage, especially given his mother's sad history with both Lavien and James Hamilton" (Bloomsbury 80). He did want companionship, however, and famously wrote to his friend John Laurens describing the perfect mate:

> She must be young, good looking, shapely—I'm very insistent on a good shape. Sensible, well bred, but not someone who puts on airs. Chaste and tender. As for money, well, it seems to be an essential ingredient to happiness in this world, and as I don't have any now and am not likely to get much of my own, I hope my wife will bring at least enough to take care of her own luxuries. It doesn't matter what her politics are, I have arguments enough to convert her to my views....As to fortune, the larger stock of that the better. You know my temper and circumstances and will, therefore, pay special attention to this article in the treaty.
> Though I run no risk of going to Purgatory for my avarice, yet as money is an essential ingredient to happiness in this world—as I have not much of my own and as I am very little calculated to get more either by my address or industry; it must needs be, that my wife, if I get one, bring at least a sufficiency to cater to her own extravagencies (Fleming 219)

In 1778, Eliza was staying with a newly married Angelica in Boston. Still, no marriage proposals arrived, and she went off to visit her aunt and uncle at the military camp at Morristown, New Jersey for the winter of 1780. Her former crush, Tench Tilghman would be there, along with many other officers. There, she found Hamilton (whom she had met in the fall of 1777) and they became entranced. He was twenty-five; she was twenty-two. Of course, many regarded her as a charmer. One of their acquaintances called her "a Brunette with the most good-natured, lively dark eyes...which threw a beam of good temper and Benevolence over her whole countenance" (Mazzeo 25).

The ball was the setting for her and Hamilton's relationship to begin. Miranda notes, "By wrapping the song around the word 'Helpless,' we encapsulate several things: the giddy helplessness of falling in love, but also Hamilton's fear of helplessness of falling in love, but also Hamilton's fear of his helplessness, and his identification of helplessness in the first woman he ever knew, his mother" As he adds of Mrs. Hamilton, and relationships with women in general, "It's a weak point for him, it's Kryptonite. And it'll come back in the form of another character in Act Two. Stay tuned" (Miranda 77). With the conventions of a pop song, Miranda shows eighteenth century social rules –the woman must not be too forward but allow the man to do the courting, even if marriage was the goal for both parties. Meanwhile, Hamilton's issues and flirtatiousness leave Eliza "helpless" to respond in kind.

The most brilliant social season of the army of the Revolution was at Morristown, the winter of '79 and '80. It was a pleasant region, as we know it today, and the society of the country made a find background for the military and foreign nobles brought there by the exigencies of the war" (Humphreys 169). Mrs. Washington presided, pointedly dressed in thrifty homespun as a picture of simple dignity. There she had her tomcat Hamilton, with thirteen stripes around the tail that suggested the continental flag, as *Rivington's Gazette* reported (Humphreys 173).

"Hamilton was girl crazy and brimming with libido. Throughout his career, at unlikely moments, he tended to grow flirtatious, even giddy, with women" (Chernow 93). The young couple flirted in her Aunt Gertrude's parlor, and when her father visited, Alexander applied for Eliza's hand— Angelica's elopement had hurt Eliza's parents enough that she considered running away unthinkable.

HAMILTON'S WOMEN

Betsey, as he soon began to call her, was petite, submissive, alluring, and the daughter of a rich and powerful New Yorker. She was everything that Hamilton had wished for. He found her attractive, especially her "fine black eyes," and he was captivated by her beauty, frankness, "innocent simplicity," "good hearted" nature, and the "sweet softness and delicacy" of her "mind and manners." He told Laurens she was "not a genius," but she had "sense enough to be agreeable." He told Betsey that she had "a lovely form" and "a mind still more lovely." Nothing was more important than her "tenderness to me," which he probably had never experienced from a woman. Hamilton spoke of the "apprehensive... nature of [his] love," perhaps an admission that he was far from the self-assured paramour that he wished others to think. Or, he may simply have worried that things might not work out, especially as he could not get away to see her. They were engaged by the time she left camp late in the spring, but he did not see her again for seven months. He had often criticized other officers who left the army when an action might occur, and he would not consider such a step. In the early stages of their separation, he brooded over the meaning of her every phrase, each lapse in her correspondence, and the ever-present possibility of a rival suitor in Albany. He reminded her of his virtues—"I have talents and a good heart" but acknowledged his shortcomings, including his immodesty and lack of i wealth. He was not the most handsome man, he added, but he would bestow on her "a heart fraught" (Bloomsbury 81)

Eliza's father was incredibly wealthy, meeting Hamilton's criteria. There was also his political influence. "Hamilton's Elizabeth was an heiress, the daughter of an upstate squire, Philip Schuyler, with Livingston and van Rensselaer connections" (Kennedy 59). Beyond this, the large family and stable home likely felt like a haven for wandering Hamilton. "For Hamilton, Eliza formed part of a beautiful package labeled 'the Schuyler family' and he spared no effort over time to ingratiate himself...The daughters in particular—all smart, beautiful, gregarious and rich—must have been the stuff of fantasy for Hamilton," Chernow comments (129). Still, this was not regarded as a bad match on the Schuylers' part. The two men had much in common. "Both Hamilton and Schuyler spoke French, were well-read, appreciated military discipline, and had a common interest in business and internal-development schemes such as canals. They also shared a common loyalty to Washington and impatience with congressional incompetence" (Chernow 135).

Further, Hamilton was Washington's right-hand man, eventually entrusted with a command. He had not yet finished college or passed the bar, but his energy and intelligence suggested he would go far and be instrumental in shaping the country, as indeed he was. Several of Burr's biographers have repeated the saw that "the Clintons had power, the Livingstons had numbers, the Schuylers had Hamilton." (Kennedy 59). Philip came to admire him and wrote to Eliza two years later, "I daily experience the pleasure of hearing encomiums on his virtue and abilities from those who are capable of distinguishing between real and pretended merit. He is considered, as he certainly is, the ornament of his country" (Chernow 136-137).

Her parents gave their consent, and she went home to prepare for the wedding, while Alexander continued at war. The couple wrote loving letters—he wrote more often than she and occasionally suggested she should study more to improve her eloquence. Chernow notes there was a reason for her reticence: "Her spelling was poor and she didn't write with the fluency of the other Schuylers" (131). She was quiet but clearly felt a great deal. "Perhaps the real-life Eliza worried her letters couldn't match his eloquence. Few could. Hamilton's missives are exquisite—lyrical, laced with classical references, angsty idealism, braggadocio, and an endearing vulnerability," Elliott notes. Still, she showed her own love with quieter tokens, sending him neckwear and cockades she had made.

"Helpless" is Eliza's romantic song, though there's a tinge of irony as with Angelica's follow-up. Eliza stresses through the song how she is dependent on the whims of her sister and father as well as Hamilton himself, as the former two have the power to take him away from her. However, in the course of the song, she chooses the man she wants for himself—

HAMILTON'S WOMEN

while Hamilton is cast as the prey for the two sisters to choose between, despite his arrogant posturing at the song's beginning. Eliza also ends the song fully "satisfied," unlike conflicted Angelica and unlike Hamilton, who retains the memory of his awkward flirtation with her sister.

The spinning of herself and the dancers on the turntable suggests being swept off her feet and having limited power here. More obviously, Eliza is so shy she must send her livelier sister to bring Hamilton over. Historically, Eliza was "the most self-effacing 'founding mother,' doing everything in her power to focus the spotlight exclusively on her husband" (Chernow 130). In his first letter to Peggy, Hamilton describes Eliza's beauty but also her "good sense" As he adds, "She has good nature affability and vivacity unembellished with that charming frivolousness which is justly deemed one of the principal accomplishments of a belle" (Villegas 80). She explains of her predicament in "Helpless": "I have never been the type to try and grab the spotlight." For this, she enlists her sister.

Hamilton writes to Eliza and asks her frankly, "Tell me my pretty damsel have you made up your mind on the subject of housekeeping? Do you soberly relish the pleasure of being a poor man's wife? Have you learned to think a home spun preferable to a brocade and the rumbling of a wagon wheel to the musical rattling of a coach and six?" (Villegas 83). On the show he asks her this after they're already married, taking some agency from her and using the argument to push his desire for promotion and glory. Still, Eliza, in both cases, is happy to live humbly.

Hamilton's fellow aide-de-camp, Tench Tilghman, aptly dubbed Eliza "the little saint of the Revolution." Tilghman also regarded this as a love match. "Hamilton," Tilghman wrote a mutual friend, "is a gone man." (Fleming 220). Meanwhile, Eliza spoke proudly of Hamilton's "Elasticity of mind. Variety of his knowledge. Playfulness of his wit. Excellence of his heart. His immense forbearance [and] virtues" (Chernow 132).

VALERIE ESTELLE FRANKEL

By February 1780, Hamilton was writing to Peggy that "by some odd contrivance or other your sister has found out the secret of interesting me in everything that concerns her" (Villegas 79). He was soon writing sweetly impassioned letters to his Betsey in which he told her, "You engross my thoughts too entirely ... You not only employ my mind all day, but you intrude on my sleep. I meet you in every dream." In another, he praised "the sweet softness and delicacy of your mind and manners, the elevation of your sentiments, the real goodness of your heart" (Fleming 220). Considering that both Angelica and Peggy eloped, Hamilton can be seen as choosing the steadier, more obedient sister—likely in a reaction to the uncertainty and tempestuousness of his own upbringing. As he wrote to Laurens:

> Have you not heard that I am on the point of becoming a benedict [a newly engaged or married man who had long been a bachelor]? I confess my sins. I am guilty. Next fall completes my doom. I give up my liberty to Miss Schuyler. She is a good hearted girl who I am sure will never play the termagant; though not a genius she has good sense enough to be agreeable, and though not a beauty, she has fine black eyes —is rather handsome and has every other requisite of the exterior to make a lover happy. And believe me, I am lover in earnest, though I do not speak of the perfections of my Mistress in the enthusiasm of Chivalry. (*Papers of Alexander Hamilton*, vol. 2, p. 347-348).

On December 14, 1780, she and Hamilton were married in her family home. Eliza's wedding present for her new husband, a fantastically embroidered picture frame around an oval watercolor of him, symbolized how she would use her talents embellishing and showing off his best features. Angelica was present, but not her husband. George and Martha Washington sent gifts and good wishes. Hamilton brought no family of his own and only one close friend, surgeon James "Mac" McHenry, who wrote of meeting Eliza, "Hers was a strong character with its depth and warmth, whether of feeling or temper controlled, but glowing underneath, bursting though at times in some emphatic expression" (Mazzeo 89).

They stayed with the family for a few weeks, visiting rela-

HAMILTON'S WOMEN

tives and letting Hamilton settle in with his new relations. After the New Year, Alexander set off for camp and joined General Washington's headquarters at New Windsor on January 11, 1781. "Eliza set off from Albany two days later, bringing with her trunks filled with wedding linens, gowns, and a few good pieces of silver, traveling more slowly and more comfortably, by boat and then carriage" (Mazzeo 90).

Onstage, meeting, courting, and marrying pass in a single hasty song. "There's a swirl of letters being sent and delivered which feels like more of the joyful ball choreography, swirling into the wedding as her sisters veil Eliza. The courtship and wedding are both balls with the swirling turntable, couple's letters, and flashback adding to the ever-spinning blur" (Frankel). Next, the musical moves on to Angelica's version of events and then back to the men and their war.

After this, Eliza next appears when she writes Hamilton's boss, George Washington himself, and requests that he sends Hamilton home, which he does. In these moments, she casts herself as a decided shaper of the story. In history, she was living with her husband at the time, but a hotheaded Hamilton still resigned over not getting a command. Suddenly, Eliza had at home an unhappy and unemployed spouse. Then Alexander let her know that he was sending her back to Albany as he couldn't afford to support her there. Eventually, he joined her.

During the war, Eliza helped in small ways, gathering supplies for the troops, dancing at balls, and listening for intelligence. She was absolutely one of the country's founding mothers, though a quiet one. "After Eliza and Hamilton marry, Eliza begs him, 'Let me be a part of the narrative,' wanting him to include her in his piece of history; tagging along with him seems to be her only option. But as Eliza grows and soon endures numerous hardships, she takes on the agency to guide her own story, navigating how to build the narrative for herself, as she moves from the edges of the story to center stage" (Corey).

VALERIE ESTELLE FRANKEL

> True, he had told his wife that marriage had "intirely changed" him, stripping away "all the public and splendid passions," leaving him "absorbed" only with his family. But more than anything, Hamilton during the spring and summer of 1781 appears to have been conflicted, torn between a desire to be with his family and an enduring passion for acclaim. If he did write to Washington, it was probably as a last effort to persuade the commander to give him a field command. (Bloomsbury 119)

At last, Hamilton received one in history and in the show. "Though I know my Betsy would be happy to hear I had rejected this proposal," Alexander chided gently in his letters, "... I hope my beloved Betsy will dismiss all apprehensions for my safety" (Mazzeo 98). Eliza appears on the ramparts during the battle, symbolically watching and worrying while also reminding Hamilton he has a responsibility to return to her. "My Eliza's expecting me/not only that, my Eliza's expecting," he sings, playing on the words and viewing her as a source of responsibility.

Of course, Hamilton survived the war and came home to his wife and child.

> After several weeks of rest, Eliza and Alexander then moved into a small farm owned by her parents, not far from the Pastures, where the new young family happily threw themselves into housekeeping. Alexander confessed to a friend, "You cannot imagine how entirely domestic I am growing. I lose all taste for the pursuits of ambition, I sigh for nothing but the company of my wife and my baby." He cast aside his law books and his papers, sat by the fire rocking the cradle, and turned his mind to sorting out their glassware and china. He was putting together a little wine cellar and planned some elegant entertaining. Could an acquaintance help him find four pint-size wine decanters? A dozen wineglasses? Beer tumblers? Eliza sorted little jars of seeds and planned for springtime and their vegetable garden. There on their little farm, they spent the winter nesting. (Mazzeo 106).

He also studied to pass the bar and set up a law practice in order to support his young family. Both in-laws were happy having them near, and included them in their domestic circle. "This was probably the happiest period of Catherine Schuyler's life....To General Schuyler, Hamilton was not a more beloved son than a valued friend and political ally. His chivalrous manner and devotion to her daughter was exceedingly agreeable to the reserved tastes of Mrs. Schuyler and to her tenderness as a mother. Here their first child was born," her biography explains (Humphreys 198).

ELIZA AS WIFE AND FOUNDING MOTHER

Onstage, Eliza is a bit of a nag though also devotedly supportive. When she asks him to give up his ambition and stay by her side repeatedly through the story, she becomes an obstacle for ambitious Alexander, and even arguably for the founding of the country. Her requests are something Alexander must navigate around in order to achieve his success. This, too, casts the story as masculine centered and dwelling on the men's view of history.

Still, it's significant that she chooses the man she wants and gets the life she wants—something Angelica's actress is sure her character admired. "I think the women that come across the most powerful are the ones that are the most aware of where real power is," Goldsberry said. "I think that Angelica is the most aware that Eliza has the most of it, even though her demeanor might not demand the same kind of attention from the beginning" (Purcell).

Still, she pursues her dreams, modest though they are, and cares for her family. "Feminism exists in the big moves toward equality, the passing of legislation and the organized movements. But it also happens in the in-between moments, the nitty-gritty of female-identifying people claiming agency and equality on a day-to-day basis, even in the face of adversity. And this is exactly what *Hamilton* gets right," Corey explains. She ran the household so efficiently that an associate told Hamilton she "has as much merit as your treasurer as you have as treasurer of the wealth of the United States"

VALERIE ESTELLE FRANKEL

("Elizabeth Hamilton").

> Like her husband, Eliza was frugal and industrious, even if often appareled in the rich clothes of a society lady. Skilled in many domestic arts, she made handbags and pot holders, arranged flowers and wove table mats, designed patterns for furniture, cooked sweetmeats and pastry, and sewed undergarments for the children. She served plentiful meals of mutton, fowl, and veal, garnished with generous portions of potatoes and turnips and topped off with fresh apples and pears. The Hamiltons were treated to fresh produce shipped regularly from Albany by the Schuylers, and there were always demijohns of good wine on hand. (Chernow 204)

Likewise, Hamilton was an attentive father to his eight children, devoting himself to their education and welfare while also taking solace in family life. Hamilton's son James wrote, "His gentle nature rendered his house a most joyous one to his children and friends...His intercourse with his children was always affectionate and confiding, which excited in them a corresponding confidence and devotion" (Villegas 5).

Sometimes Eliza even got her way: Hamilton wrote to Angelica that he had resigned his seat in the Cabinet in 1795. "To indulge my domestic happiness more freely was the primary motive for relinquishing an office in which it is said I have gained some glory, and the difficulties of which had just been subdued. Eliza and her children are here with me at your father's house, who is himself in New York attending the Legislature. We remain here until June, when we become stationary at New York, where I resume the practice of law. For, my dear sister, I tell you without regret what I hope you anticipate, that I am poorer than I went into office. I allot myself four or five years of work than will be pleasant, though much less than I have had for the last five years" (Humphreys 232-232)

Through it all, she managed their home, wherever it was located. "Betsey had excellent taste. She decorated their various homes with Louis XIV-style chairs and portraits by the best painters. Her dresses were stylish and beautifully cut. Her

HAMILTON'S WOMEN

model was Martha Washington" (Fleming 237). Firm and affectionate as a mother, Elizabeth made sure her children had a religious upbringing. She raised them to be mindful and well-educated. On the show, she's seen mediating for young Philip on his ninth birthday, insisting her husband stop working and attend their son's small rap performance while she beat-boxes for him. She's seen instructing him in French and piano, her own skills.

She moved in social circles with his husbands and fellow politicians—"Burr and Hamilton supped at each other's homes, and Burr's wife, Theodosia, visited Eliza" (Chernow 191). Other acquaintances, Eliza liked better. "There were daily playdates with the Washington family, and the children were in and out of both homes constantly. Twice a week, the president's elegant carriage stopped in the lane and four of the youngsters—Angelica, Fanny, Felly, and Wash—rolled off to dancing lessons under the kindly eye of Martha Washington. In the afternoons, when he wanted some peace and quiet, George Washington came to sit in Eliza's parlor and read the newspaper or watch the children play" (Mazzeo 153). Likewise, cousins and extended family were always coming and going as the larger part of her own household. Further, she raised a friend's orphaned daughter alongside her own children for a decade. The Hamiltons also fostered John Bradstreet's son and Lafayette's son, seeing to the education of each while in New York.

As Eliza saw friends' children orphaned and friends tossed into debtor's prison, she resolved to reform the system and find other options for the destitute. Alexander proposed she actually go to debtor's prison to sit for the incarcerated artist, Ralph Earl, could paint his way to freedom. One of the Hamilton sons remembered later, their father asked their mother to go "to the debtors' jail to sit for her portrait and she induced other ladies to do the same" (Mazzeo 120). This, her most famous portrait, thus helped to save the artist.

Earl saw Betsey as an attractive women, with deep-set dark eyes under thick brows. She is stylishly dressed and coiffed. But her

VALERIE ESTELLE FRANKEL

> tentative smile conveys an impression of insecurity, even melancholy. There is not a trace of the energy and self-confidence that emanates from almost every portrait of her husband. Betsey s portrait was painted in 1787. By that time, Alexander Hamilton had closed his military career by persuading George Washington to give him command of a light infantry regiment at the siege of Yorktown, where he led a charge that made him a popular hero. After the war he emerged as one of New York's most successful lawyers and a political thinker of formidable stature. He played a crucial role in persuading Americans to junk their unworkable first constitution, the Articles of Confederation, and create a new national charter. Riding this political whirlwind absorbed most of Hamilton's waking hours. (Fleming 224)

Eliza was pregnant nine times between 1781 and 1802, and lost one child to miscarriage. The dozens of letters her husband sent to her during the war and his time in political office reveal a tender love and an implicit trust in her as a confidante. As the pressure of political life increased, Hamilton often expressed a melancholy loneliness in Eliza's absence and increasing dependence on her support. She actively helped him with his work. For instance, as he wrote all night for his central banking system, she worked beside him at home: As Eliza described Alexander's role and vision from 1790 after the fact, "He made your government. ... He made your bank. I sat up all night with him to help him do it. Jefferson thought we ought not to have a bank and President Washington thought so. But my husband said, 'We must have a Bank.' I sat up all night, copied out his writing, and the next morning, he carried it to President Washington and we had a bank" (Mazzeo 140).

At the inaugural ball, Eliza was one of the few ladies asked to dance by President Washington. Martha Washington considered her a close friend and protégé. "I mingled ... in the gaieties of the day," Eliza recalled. "I was at the inauguration ball—the most brilliant of them all" (Mazzeo 130).

Eliza is far more equanimical than Hamilton—her song, "That Would Be Enough" smacks of satisfaction, unlike the ambition in her sister and husband. Her quest is to help Hamilton see her perspective and be satisfied, whereas he

HAMILTON'S WOMEN

climbs the moving ladder away from her in "Non-Stop" to serve his ambition. In "Schuyler Defeated," she sings, "Sometimes that's how it goes," emphasizing her willingness to not worry over setbacks. "Eliza escapes the suffering of Hamilton by recognizing that everything changes, and that we should enjoy what time we have here and take what comes without striving to keep everything from changing. For Alexander, both his story and Eliza's story are one narrative dealing with the same triumphs and tragedies." (Ross 119-120). Alexander's ego dominates, while Eliza accepts life philosophically. In fact, Alexander's refusal to take a break as Eliza insists leads to his being stressed, overworked, and lonely—the show's excuse for Alexander's infidelity. Only when his son is killed does he learn to give up on affecting the world and simply let it pass. He sings his own version of "That Would Be Enough" back to Eliza, showing that he's finally reached her view.

In Act 2, Eliza begins suffering as more than a neglected wife when she finds out about Hamilton's affair with Maria Reynolds that summer. The public humiliation matches a private betrayal as she sadly sings, "I thought you were mine." Historically, a hostile press asked, "Art thou a wife? See him, whom thou has chosen for the partner of this life, lolling in the lap of a harlot!!" ("Elizabeth Hamilton"). Thus mocked in the paper, Eliza had handed it to John Barker Church with a gesture of contemptuous dismissal. Church had told Hamilton that the accusation "made not the least impression on her" (Fleming 243).

Hamilton turned attentive and penitent. He devotedly nursed fifteen-year-old Philip through a bout of typhoid until his recovery. Meanwhile, Eliza retreated to her parents' house for a time. In history and show, divorce was not a choice— not religiously or socially, and not with a crowd of children to support. Eventually, she forgave her husband and they had more children—their next was named Elizabeth, likely in a husband's gesture of devotion to his wife.

Onstage, she takes a different revenge. Dramatically in a

vulnerable white undergown, all alone and blue-lit on a dark stage, she lights her love letters on actual fire, depriving him of her words of love and the sentiments behind them. "In a simple white gown, suggesting innocence and vulnerability with its low neckline and brief blue sash, Eliza kneels as if at an altar praying. There's a single lantern on the white stone gravelike bench beside her" (Frankel).

"I'm burning the memories/Burning the letters that might have redeemed you," she sings. Historically, her burning the letters was reportedly done for privacy, a choice many famous people made upon realizing they would become a significant part of history. Her burning her own letters but preserving her husband's could be viewed as self-effacing (literally taking herself out of the narrative to focus on him) or shy, but there is no particular reason to consider it vindictive. However, this reframing in the musical gives her an angry, sorrowful response in which she considers how much Hamilton's charm has been based in lies. Further, when Eliza burns the letters, she claims agency over her own history. "The musical's Eliza Hamilton is a complex and sophisticated woman, and not a passive, two-dimensional caricature," Timm observes (203). As she explains:

I'm erasing myself from the narrative.
Let future historians wonder
how Eliza reacted when you broke her heart.

Worse follows, as the scandal leads Philip to challenge a young man to a duel and get killed in the process—another betrayal compounded by the first as a horrified Eliza demands of her husband, "Did you know?" "Never did I see a man so completely overwhelmed with grief as Hamilton has been," Robert Troup wrote after. "The scene I was present at, when Mrs. Hamilton came to see her son on his deathbed (he died about a mile out of the city) and when she met her husband and son in one room, beggars all description!" Thomas Rathbone's description of how Eliza and Alexander passed that night is equally striking: "On a Bed without curtains lay poor Phil, pale and languid, his rolling, distorted eye balls darting f6rth the flashes of delirium—on one side of him on the same bed lay his agonized father—on the other his distracted mother. Holding their son between them, their hands touching, Eliza and Alexander lay together until just before dawn, when Philip stopped breathing" (Mazzeo 220). She was three months pregnant.

If a masculine approach to the world is ambitious, adversarial, and hierarchal, it's clearly Hamilton's life model. He is indeed a soldier, tomcat, politician, and man's man. By contrast, Angelica and Eliza both show an ethic of care. Indeed, Hamilton's masculinist world kills his son then himself, even as his pride pushes him to publish the Reynolds Pamphlet, ignoring his duties and love for his family. "The contrasting songs 'Stay Alive'—the first about winning a war, and the second highlighting the foolishness of dueling as Philip has died for a clumsy, immature, boyish honor, contrast masculine and feminine values" (Dobrick 181-182). Dobrick notes how difficult Hamilton finds it to straddle these conflicting sets of values: "Alexander advises Philip to aim at the sky, thus not losing his honor or his life, simultaneously trying to protect him from the masculinist value system while also feeling the need to embrace it by engaging in a duel" (182). As Dobrick continues, Eliza continues to cling to her own feminine approach to the world:

> Eliza's ethic of care was truly tested. She faced her son's death because of a botched attempt to defend Alexander's manly honor. This happened after Alexander did his best to destroy his honor with Maria Reynolds. Eliza eventually forgives, and then steadfastly supports, her husband. We learn of Eliza's lifelong dedication to Alexander's story after his untimely death in yet another masculinist, violent duel. Her description of the orphanage she builds in Hamilton's memory brings listeners to tears. Founding the orphanage brings the ethic of care to its logical conclusion: Eliza gives of herself for the sake of orphans, for no other reason than to have meaningful relationships and to help these children in unfortunate circumstances. The tears that the words "The Orphanage" elicit are testaments to the emotional appreciation and human connection we often feel toward

VALERIE ESTELLE FRANKEL

> philanthropists and social activists who practice real-life applications of the ethics of care. (182-183)

In history, this was compounded by her daughter Angelica's succumbing to a mental illness from which she never recovered. Eliza cared for her too.

> Eliza's grandson Allan McLane Hamilton wrote decades later that "upon receipt of the news of her brother's death in the Packer duel, [Angelica Hamilton] suffered so great a shock that her mind became permanently impaired" with something he called "insanity." But the truth was sadder and more complicated. Philip's funeral and the family's despair tipped the scales in what had already been a precarious balance, and the underlying condition was probably schizophrenia. What is certain is that the trauma of her brother's death triggered psychosis and sent the seventeen-year-old young woman into a spiral. Sometimes Angelica lived in a world in which Philip had not died, and Eliza listened, heart heavy, as she played the same old songs from their childhood obsessively. Sometimes she became withdrawn and catatonic, and Eliza could not reach her daughter. Other times, Alexander and Eliza caught glimpses of the old Angelica and dared to believe things would get better. And sometimes, for a while, they did. Hope was agony for Eliza. (Mazzeo 221)

On the show, Philip mentions the presence of a sister, but she is not identified as little Angelica specifically, nor are her mental issues addressed.

Afterwards, Eliza heroically gets past her anger and forgives Alexander (as the Company sings beautifully, "Forgiveness. Can you imagine?"). Hamilton's "Look around, look around," is very bittersweet—acknowledging a moment of grief not happiness but also trying to see the city through her point of view—a wondrous place. For the first time, he's passive, admiring the world around them instead of fighting to change it. Likewise, Hamilton's reprise of Eliza's "That Would Be Enough" at the end of "It's Quiet Uptown" is more than an apology—he emphasizes that he sees her worldview and will give himself over to it at last. Using her melody and words, he emphasizes that he's ready to set aside his boundless ambition:

> But I'm not afraid
> I know who I married

HAMILTON'S WOMEN

> Just let me stay here by your side
> That would be enough

The new paradise he envisions is much like Eliza's during the first version of this song—the pair of them staying at home raising their children. Before this, he has never suggested anything would be "enough" to stop him from seeking further advancement. Saying "I don't pretend to know" also represents a significant departure for Hamilton—he's always had an answer he was sure of, even when, in the case of the Reynolds Pamphlet, circumstances proved him wrong. This emotional territory, however, is not only shocking for him but new, an area where he realizes Eliza is better skilled. However, he's "not afraid" to come to her like this, since he "knows who he married" and knows he can trust her to make the best choice for them. They stand in the same garden where Eliza reached out to him with "That Would Be Enough" and then grieved the blow to their marriage in "Burn." This is her territory, her place of power. He wishes he could trade his life for Philip's, trying to make amends. However, this line just foreshadows his death and emphasizes that sacrificing himself is not a solution. Alexander forgets that Eliza's one desire for her men is to "come home at the end of the day," and for that, they have to "stay alive."

After Phillip's death, Alexander puts his hand over Eliza's, but she violently removes her hand, disgusted. Here, she finally takes Alexander's hand, accepting his apology. His use of "we" shows that he's empathizing with her pain even as he tells her that bringing Philip back to make her smile would satisfy him. He suggests a new, far quieter plan—a new house and new start where they can stay with the children, distant from the politics and responsibilities of downtown New York. He will be happy sharing family life where "It's quiet uptown." She repeats this last line to him, accepting this olive branch and a life together. She has received what she always wanted, and by singing here, she puts herself back in the narrative. The chiming piano chords before Eliza sings for the first time in this song recall the opening of "Yorktown": That moment signals a new beginning, as does this one. It's logical to tie this into the story here—the prospect of a change and a house built to suit Eliza, farther from the bustle of the city as a token of comfort for her. In the quiet of their loss, husband and wife finally can connect.

Historically, the house was already begun. "By the late 1790s, the Harlem Heights area was a popular summer retreat for the city's wealthy...Far from the gossip, unburdened by tedious social calls and the dictates of city customs, [Eliza] laughed with their children and spent long, delightful hours riding through the fields again and growing flowers. Unlike the other city husbands, Alexander joined his wife there" (Mazzeo 206). He saw her relaxed and happy at last. In November, he arranged a surprise for her. In an upbeat and flirtatious letter, Alexander wrote to Eliza:

> You are my good genius; of that kind which the ancient Philosophers called a familiar; and you know very well that I am glad to be in every way as familiar as possible with you. I have formed a sweet project, of which I will make you my confidant when I come to New York, and in which I rely that you will cooperate with me chearfully. "You may guess and guess and guess again Your guessing will be still in vain. But you will not be the less pleased when you come to understand and realize the scheme. Adieu best of wives & best of mothers. Heaven ever bless you & me in you. (Mazzeo 207)

As Mazzeo adds, "The letter is a rare peek at the heart of their marriage, and it is not a glimpse into, a marriage struggling with betrayal. It is a letter that speaks of Alexander's love, of their continued intimacy, and offers his thanks, in the private language of their relationship, for Eliza's sacrifice and loyalty" (207). The family began building a grand house (though one that Alexander could not yet afford).

When Eliza gave birth to another little boy on June 2, after her oldest son's death, they named him Philip after his lost brother. "May the loss of one be compensated by another Philip," wrote her father. "May his virtues emulate those which graced his brother, and may he be a comfort to parents so tender" (Mazzeo 222).

HAMILTON'S WOMEN

On June 27, Burr sent a formal challenge. Onstage, Hamilton bids his wife a brief but touching goodbye before the duel, calling her "the best of wives and the best of women." This song is set to the same melancholy instrumental as "It's Quiet Uptown," emphasizing their sad yet improved relationship. His actual final letter to her is also quite touching:

> [New York, July 4, 1804]
>
> This letter, my very dear Eliza, will not be delivered to you, unless I shall first have terminated my earthly career; to begin, as I humbly hope from redeeming grace and divine mercy, a happy immortality.
>
> If it had been possible for me to have avoided the interview, my love for you and my precious children would have been alone a decisive motive. But it was not possible, without sacrifices which would have rendered me unworthy of your esteem. I need not tell you of the pangs I feel, from the idea of quitting you and exposing you to the anguish which I know you would feel. Nor could I dwell on the topic lest it should unman me.
>
> The consolations of Religion, my beloved, can alone support you; and these you have a right to enjoy. Fly to the bosom of your God and be comforted. With my last idea; I shall cherish the sweet hope of meeting you in a better world.
>
> Adieu best of wives and best of Women. Embrace all my darling Children for me.
>
> Ever yours
>
> A H (Papers of Alexander Hamilton, vol. 26, p. 293)

A day later, Eliza's beloved husband, like her oldest son, was dead. This was one of many shocking blows around this time. Peggy had died in 1801, and soon Peggy's widowed husband shocked the family with a hasty remarriage. "In August, Angelica's eleven-year-old boy, Alexander, came down with the influenza that swept the city that summer. For two weeks, the doctors bled the little boy in a futile attempt to drain the fevers, until he finally perished. Eliza sat for a long time in darkened rooms with Angelica after the men carried away the small body" (Mazzeo 223). On March 7, 1803, Eliza's mother Kitty suffered a massive stroke and died within minutes. Her father Philip died in Albany on November 18, 1804, four months after Alexander Hamilton's duel. It was a very bad few years for the family.

VALERIE ESTELLE FRANKEL

There was also the financial burden. Hamilton's death left Eliza supporting seven children with so little money that she was forced to sell the Grange at auction, to her great dismay. Her friends took up a collection to help her, but her father's death and the division of his own estate left her with very little.

> After it was all said and done, by spring Eliza was left with an inheritance of $15,000—less than $300,000 today. It was nowhere near enough to allow her to dream of buying back the Grange from Alexander's creditors. Their home went on the auction block at last and sold for $30,000. Eliza took the news calmly, but her heart ached when she turned her back for the last time and walked away from the home she and Alexander had built together. What she did not know was that behind the sale lay a marvelous secret. Alexander's friends knew how hard she and the children had taken leaving the Grange, and they had searched for a way to show their affection, too, for Alexander and his family—a way that would give the family back some kind of equilibrium. So a group of them, including her brother-in-law Washington Morton, banded together, and, when the Grange went under the hammer, put up the money together to buy it. They wanted to sell it back to Eliza. They would take for a price the $15,000 she had in her savings. Eliza was humbled and deeply grateful. (Mazzeo 246)

She also pressured Congress for her husband's war pay—gallantly refused but vital for her to live on. In the spring of 1816, Congress passed at last An Act for the Relief of Elizabeth Hamilton, awarding her "five years' full pay for the services of her deceased husband." With over thirty years of interest, "the total sum was $10,609.64, and for Eliza it was life changing. She was not a wealthy woman. But she would be able to live in quiet comfort as a widow and provide for her daughter Angelica's care and for the education of her three youngest children" (Mazzeo 257).

Eliza's Legacy

At the end of the show, Eliza decides to "put myself back in the narrative" and offers an account of her life, which continued for 50 years after Hamilton's death. She becomes an activist, "speak[ing] out against slavery" and founding "the first private orphanage in New York City." She and Angelica gather Hamilton's letters, and "I try to make sense of your thousands of pages of writing," in order to write his story, to write this story. The supremely intelligent and self-reflexive musical ends with a commentary on the very writing of history, underlining the importance of the author. "Who lives, who dies, who tells your story?" repeats the Company. In the end, *Hamilton* reveals, all of this exists because of Eliza (and Angelica), her efforts, and her own ability to write and to tell his life's narrative. She is the author. (Wolf)

First, Eliza elevated Hamilton's status through marriage. After his death, she worked for the rest of her life to preserve what he had created. This was all done within the confines of what the Colonial world gave her permission to accomplish as a woman, though out of love, she did far more than many of her peers. "Without Eliza's dedication to living out the ethic of care, where would Alexander's devotion to the masculinist ethic of justice have left his precious legacy," Dobrick asks (180). It's Eliza and Angelica's devotion that makes it happen.

Of course, Eliza's position as Founding Mother enhanced this duty: "In a selfish sense, it was in her interest to have a positive legacy for her husband. Her life was intertwined with his. When he looked good, she looked good. Also, she loved him," as Andy Wible notes in his essay on legacy (96). Without her devotion to organizing his papers, Hamilton could easily have been relegated to the trash-heap of political scandal or overlooked as a Founding Father. Indeed, in a world in which Hamilton had been publicly slurred, with Jefferson and

VALERIE ESTELLE FRANKEL

then Madison as presidents determined to control the narrative, she had a great deal to do, protecting and even enlarging Alexander Hamilton's reputation as one of the founders of the American republic.

> Eliza Hamilton set herself the task of collecting her husband's papers. She devoted many hours to retrieving copies of the hundreds of letters he had written to friends and supporters. She even persuaded the Washington family to let her borrow and copy Hamilton's letters to the president. She interviewed politicians who had worked with Hamilton and added memoranda of their memories to her files. For the next twenty years, she tried to persuade one of Hamilton's friends or admirers to write his biography. She met with one frustration after another. Various prominent politicians and writers studied the papers for years at a time and then returned them, pleading ill health or advancing age. A climactic disappointment was the failure of former secretary of state Timothy Pickering. He kept the papers for almost a decade. When he died in 1829, his heirs found only a few disjointed, unfinished chapters. By this time Eliza's second-oldest son, John Church Hamilton, was ready to undertake the task, and he began his seven-volume *History of the Republic Traced in the Writings of Hamilton,* which would consume the next thirty years of his life. (Fleming 253)

As the musical says, she lived another fifty years and found ways to make herself a heroine and protector for the most desperate during that time. "I don't find it surprising that she lived to be 97-years-old," Phillipa Soo said of Eliza, adding, "She knew that she had a purpose" (Semigran). She never remarried and continued to dress in mourning. "This devotion to her husband's memory was by no means the only thing that occupied Eliza Hamilton. Long regarded as a fragile, dependent woman, she began demonstrating an independence and originality that amazed everyone. All her life Eliza had been dominated by strong-willed men, first her father, then her husband" (Fleming 254). Now, at last, she was free to choose.

She joined a group of religious women and with them founded The New York Orphan Asylum Society. "She learned to know and care about each of the 158 children then

HAMILTON'S WOMEN

in residence in the building the society had erected in Greenwich Village. She helped them get jobs and persuaded a New York politician to recommend one boy for West Point. Later she persuaded the New York state legislature to give the school annual grants. In 1836, she presided over a ceremony that began the construction of a larger and more permanent orphanage at Riverside Drive and 73rd Street" (Fleming 254). Eliza created this orphan asylum, the first in New York, where she worked tirelessly helping children as desperate as young Alexander Hamilton had been. She soon took the leadership role as director.

> By 1820 the facility was home to more than a hundred children; Eliza saw that need continued to outpace resources. When the orphanage was full to capacity, Eliza couldn't bear to turn a child away...so she brought them home with her. One little boy named Henry McKavit she took herself from the arms of the fireman who saved him from the burning house where his parents perished when he was five. When the time came in the next decade, despite her modest widow's budget, she personally paid for Henry's education. And that, too, got her thinking. Eliza had struggled to put her own sons through school on her meager resources as a widow. Alexander had risen in the world as an orphan only because some good-hearted souls had seen in the boy a talent worth caring about and had paid for his schooling. Education became a new charitable passion. So, through tireless fundraising and by herself donating a parcel of land on Broadway in Harlem, Eliza opened the first public school in Washington Heights. "Whole familys have been unbaptised some persons in their neighborhood have [taken] up by subscription a school," she wrote-modestly, while pressing for a donation, but "there is still about one hundred dollars wanted to complete the expenditure and to give benches and writing desks." Before long, the Hamilton Free School was open. (Mazzeo 266)

At age eighty, but still formidable and seeking new challenges, she traveled to the West to see her son William and have a grand adventure. When she made out her will, she left her widowed daughter and constant companion Betsey Holly to manage it all.

> She preferred to trust her steady, sensible, widowed daughter. She left to her sons—James, John, Alexander Jr., Philip, and Wil-

VALERIE ESTELLE FRANKEL

> liam—a mother's love. Everything else she left to her widowed daughter, in trust for the care of the orphaned Angelica, who would live "lost to her herself," as those who knew her put it, for decades. James, hurt and angry, set off for Europe in a fit of pique and stayed away for the better part of the next half decade. With the house at St. Marks Place lost to the bank following the crash, Alexander Jr. and his wife left as well again for Spain, and in 1842 Eliza's youngest son, Philip, married at last, to a young woman of abolitionist sympathies named Rebecca McLane. Philip and Rebecca, alongside Eliza's "orphan" daughter Fanny Antill and her husband, Arthur Tappan, joined the secret resistance movement known by the 1830s as the Underground Railroad. Years later, Philip's young boys remembered discovering a "very black and ragged man in the cellar who was being fed by my father himself." By the 1840s, Eliza and her daughter Betsey— now living together in a rented house on Prince Street in New York City and considering what to do next—had also embraced the cause of the abolitionists and spoke out against slavery. (Mazzeo 282)

In 1848, at the age of ninety-one, Eliza Hamilton moved to Washington, D.C., to live with Betsey. They dwelled only a few doors from the White House, where Mrs. Hamilton held court as a celebrity. Eliza's mind remained clear, and many visited her parlor to share in her living history and see the wine cooler the Washingtons had sent her. Chernow's book even begins with the elderly Eliza hosting visitors to discuss her life, emphasizing how the entire biography is largely based on her research and depiction of her husband. In Chernow's version, she would gaze longingly at her marble bust of Hamilton and express wistfully her wishes to reunite with him—a sentiment that appears at the musical's end.

President James Polk recorded in his diary a dinner party in her company in the winter of 1845, noting that "Mrs. General Hamilton, upon whom I waited at table, is a very remarkable person" (Mazzeo 284). Former president James Monroe visited to make amends for his role in revealing Alexander's sex scandal, and she actually insisted she had no time for it and asked him to leave. A woman friend described her face as "full of nerve and spirit." As she grew older, the same friend marveled at how she "retains to an astonishing degree her faculties and converses with ... ease and brilliancy" (Fleming 254).

Eliza also threw herself full-time into the work of helping her old friend First Lady Dolley Madison raise donations to build the Washington Monument. "Eliza Hamilton called on the know-how she had acquired in her forty years of lobbying and fundraising for New York's orphans. Together these two remarkable women loaned their names to a campaign to raise enough money to begin the huge task" (Fleming 255). On July 4, 1848, in a grand ceremony; the cornerstone was laid. "Eliza sat beside George Washington Parke Custis, the grandson of Martha and the general, and she could hardly believe that this was the little boy who, decades earlier, had gone to dancing lessons in Martha Washington's coach with her own young children" (Mazzeo 285).

Eliza died in 1854 at the age of ninety-seven. In a small pouch she wore around her neck, her daughter found the letter Alexander Hamilton had written to her, testifying to his transcendent love (Fleming 255). The poem was his courtship sonnet to her, romantic and tender as he tells her, "No joy unmixed my bosom warms/But when my angel's in my arms."

The musical of course summarizes all this, emphasizing Eliza as the family survivor and spokesperson, advancing Hamilton's legacy but also Washington's memory and Laurens' cause of antislavery. In the final number, she takes center stage at last. Finally, she shines as the savior and preserver of all Hamilton did through the entire show, even as her presence concludes her and Angelica's status as narrators through the story, in "Stay Alive" and "It's Quiet Uptown" as well as other numbers.

Certainly, it's arguable how feminist this depiction of her is as Eliza's true impact on history is only emphasized in the final song. Wolf decides, "On the one hand, it's a profound gesture of respect towards Eliza. But theatrically, it's too little too late. After a musical packed with non-stop movement,

VALERIE ESTELLE FRANKEL

dramatic intensity, strong melodies, and galvanizing rhythms, it's narrowly focused and understated. Though appropriate for the show's conclusion, it can't rescue Eliza or women in the musical from their inconsequential role." Michael Schulman also weighs in in his *New Yorker* article "The Women of *Hamilton*," in which he sees a deeper acknowledgement:

> Is it a feminist ending? Almost. The notion that men do the deeds and the women tell their stories isn't exactly Germaine Greer-worthy. (Look at the history-making women being considered to replace Hamilton on the ten-dollar bill.) But, in placing Eliza front and center, Miranda is reinforcing his over-all project, which is in part to displace the founding story as the province of white men. By setting the tale in a hip-hop vernacular, acted entirely by people of color (King George III is the only main character played by a white actor), Miranda is reclaiming the American story that got told—and still gets told, on currency, in statues, and in textbooks—for the people whom history habitually forgets. As a Latino working in the Broadway theatre, he knows the importance of who tells the story, and how. And, by implicitly equating Eliza's acts of narration with his own, he's acknowledging the women who built the country alongside the men. You're left wondering whether the "Hamilton" of the title isn't just Alexander but Eliza too.

PEGGY

Miranda notes, "Poor Peggy—she doesn't stick around the story long enough to merit a musical motif. She married rich and died young, in case you're wondering where she is in Act Two" (Miranda 42). Peggy, the third sister, "was from the beginning, the wildest, most high-spirited Schuyler daughter" (Mazzeo 7). She had actually been named Margarita and was accomplished at French and painting. She "was dark-haired, plump, and, some said, the prettiest of all the three sisters, with a sarcastic sense of humor that intimidated those less clever and less witty. She possessed the lion's share of family musical talent, and played the guitar with real skill and sang

HAMILTON'S WOMEN

moving ballads in a clear soprano. She also inherited her father's imperious demeanor, and she and Philip Schuyler clashed on more than one occasion. She was his willful child and, with her saucy tongue, his most exasperating daughter" (Mazzeo 25). Her mother Kitty Schuyler's biographer, Mary Gay Humphreys, described Peggy as having "animated and striking" features; as a young woman, she was "lively" and "bright, high-spirited [and] generous."

Fluent in French like Angelica, she had a romance with a French officer who was one of only eight people honored with a Congressional Medal during the Revolution, as she, like her sisters, fell for the heroes of the Revolution. She also taught herself German out of her father's engineering manuals in his massive library. Called "a wicked wit," "endowed with a rare accuracy of judgment in men and things," Peggy was a feisty "favorite at dinner tables and balls" (Elliott). One of Hamilton's closest friends, James McHenry, criticized Peggy as being a "Swift's Vanessa" –code at the time for a woman too keen on talking politics with men to be entirely desirable. "Tell her so," McHenry wrote Hamilton. "I am sure her good sense will soon place her in her proper station" (Elliott).

Though not as close with the other two as Angelica and Eliza appeared with each other, she eagerly participated in family affairs. She cared for her siblings regularly, before and after her marriage. She likewise accompanied Angelica on the dangerous trip to rejoin her husband at Yorktown, presumably to help with her children. Family friend General John Bradstreet was said to have died in teenage Peggy's soothing arms.

In the most famous story about Peggy, in the summer of 1781 (after Eliza and Angelica had married), there was an attack on the house. Her parents were there, along with her sisters and their children. Her father led them all upstairs and barricaded the door.

> Eliza never forgot the awful sound of the front door cracking as it broke open. "The attack and defense of the house was bloody and obstinate, on both sides," British officer Barry St. Leger re-

VALERIE ESTELLE FRANKEL

> ported of the mission to capture General Schuyler later. The children were hysterical by now, and in that moment a terrible realization swept over Kitty Schuyler. She had forgotten baby Catherine downstairs in the cradle. Eliza watched as her courageous mother crumbled. Kitty was on her knees. Angelica was crying. Eliza looked on in horror. Peggy took in the scene and, ever impetuous, acted. *Someone needs to get the baby.* Eliza read the thought on the face of her sister, but the wheels in her brain turned too slowly. Peggy swept her skirts up into a fist and, with a defiant flounce, turned on her heel and bolted down the staircase. Before Eliza could think to move, Peggy was already in the hallway. (Mazzeo 100)

A tomahawk, hurled at her head, left marks on the bannister that persist to this day, but she succeeded in snatching up the baby. When an attacker demanded to know where the general was, she boldly insisted he was getting reinforcements, and his men fled. Hamilton was horrified by the news and wrote to Eliza, "I have received, my beloved Betsey, your letter informing me of the happy escape of your father. He showed an admirable presence of mind...My heart...has felt all the horror and anguish attached to the idea of your being yourself and seeing your father in the power of ruffians" (Chernow 160).

> Eliza was an accomplished artist...We know that because Hamilton refers to her miniature portrait of Peggy when he writes and begs the younger Schuyler sister's help in courting Eliza. Saying he has already formed "a more than common partiality" for Peggy's "person and mind" from Eliza's painting and descriptions, Hamilton playfully begs Peggy, as a "nymph of equal sway," to come distract the other aides-de-camp so he can monopolize Eliza. That's right, in real life it was Peggy (not Angelica) who was Alexander's confidante in romancing Eliza at that fateful "Midwinter's Ball," February 1780. (Elliott)

As the musical suggests, she and Hamilton had a good relationship. "Peggy was a friend—perhaps the only woman in Hamilton's life with whom he did not engage in double entendre. Lots of affectionate teasing, yes, but very much that of a knowing big brother to a strong-willed and vivacious younger sister" (Elliott). He called her "My Peggy" in the snippets of letters that referenced her.

HAMILTON'S WOMEN

Writing to introduce himself to Peggy at Eliza's request, Hamilton described the good opinion of her Eliza had conveyed and gushed over the lovely pictures of her Eliza had drawn. As he went on, he told her boldly, "You will no doubt admit it as a full proof of my frankness and good opinion of you, that I with so little ceremony introduce myself to your acquaintance and at the first step make you my confidante" (Villegas 79). "In answer to Hamilton's letter, Peggy bodaciously rode out into the worst winter ever recorded in American history, through 4-to-6-foot snowdrifts and frost-bite cold to reach Morristown, NJ. Perhaps Peggy feared the man wooing her gentle middle sister was another dangerously charming rogue, like the man Angelica had fallen for three years earlier" (Elliott). Meanwhile, Hamilton wrote to Eliza, "Mrs. Carter [Angelica], Peggy, and yourself are the dayly toasts of our table...though as I am always thinking of you, this naturally brings Peggy to my mind who is generally my toast."

Another life-defining moment was coming for the young woman in the issue of her marriage. At twenty-five, though vivacious, pretty, and charming, she worried she would never wed. "As Peggy saw her sister off [after her wedding], she was filled with despair, frustration and perhaps, if she were honest, even a bit of jealousy at Eliza's good fortune...She was tired of being stuck at home with her mother, looking after younger siblings and managing the canning. She had her beaux, and she knew that some people said she was the prettiest of the Schuyler sisters" (Mazzeo 91).

Peggy's family likewise wondered whether she would ever find a husband. Their old family friend Benjamin Franklin asked a mutual acquaintance in 1778 if she were married yet, and he answered back, "I have not heard that the wild Miss Peggy has found a match to her liking." Peggy's sisters began advising her to be less choosy when came to marriage offers. However, Alexander, seeing she was despairing, advised her not to marry just anyone, no matter what her sisters asked her. Eliza might "persuade all her friends to embark with her on the matrimonial voyage," Alexander told Peggy, but he sounded a note of caution: "I pray you do not let her advice have so much influence as to make you matrimony-mad. Tis a very good thing when their stars unite two people who are fit for each other.... But it's a dog of life when two dissonant tempers meet, and 'tis ten to one but this is the case. When therefore I join her in advising you to marry, I add her cautions in the choice" (Mazzeo 91).

In fact, she had a dazzling match planned out. She set her eyes on her cousin, who adored her—and he was quite a catch. "Stephen Van Rensselaer was a scrawny young man. He had high, dark eyebrows; a long, thin nose; friendly eyes; an easy laugh; and extremely deep pockets. His fortune still ranks today, centuries later, as one of the largest ever in American history" (Mazzeo 109). Stephen was the oldest child of Stephen Van Rensselaer II, the ninth patroon of Rensselaerswyck, and of Catherine Livingston, daughter of Philip Livingston, a signer of the Declaration of Independence. Rensselaerswyck was a huge estate covering parts of several counties near Albany, New York. His father had died when he was five and he was brought up by guardians and trustees. He proposed on a visit out from Harvard, and she quickly accepted. However, the family were appalled and forbade the match.

> The problem with the young patroon's marriage, everyone agreed, was not Peggy Schuyler. The trouble was the youth of a teenage Stephen Van Rensselaer. In a few years, when Stephen had come of age and was no longer a minor, when his fortune was his to manage, and he had found his sense of himself as a man and estate master, then, of course, no one could object to one of General Schuyler's daughters, even "wild Miss Peggy." If Stephen felt the same way at twenty-two or twenty-three, the path was open. If. After all, crushes came and went, and young men were often fickle. But in three or four years, Peggy would be approaching thirty. If the rest of them had missed that fact, Peggy certainly hadn't. Peggy Schuyler was not about to wait years to see if the young man changed his mind and risk losing her certain chance to get a husband. Their unfortunate cousin Kiliaen Van Rensselaer was pressed into duty as a secret messenger, de-

HAMILTON'S WOMEN

> spite his protests, and Stephen set off in a boat for Saratoga. Peggy carefully folded a mauve silk gown, worked with an overskirt of damask flowers, and some of her nicest bits of lace into a satchel and, when the signal came, slipped away from their summer encampment and down to the river with her suitor. The next morning, Peggy got her wish. They eloped and were immediately married. No minister in Rensselaerwyck was going to refuse the patroon. (Mazzeo 110)

When Peggy was missing in the morning, everyone suspected the truth. Still barely reconciled with Angelica, who had been similarly bold, Philip and Kitty Schuyler were more disappointed than enraged. However, the boy's guardian, Abraham Ten Broeck, was furious, and Philip Schuyler did his best to smooth things out. In time, the young couple were forgiven. They were also quite happy. "Peggy—always the impulsive Schuyler girl—was smart, funny, haughty, beautiful, and she never tired of dancing. And he was in love with her. The couple promptly moved into a mansion in the center of Albany" (Mazzeo 111). She supported his running for and becoming lieutenant governor of New York in 1795. He also became a state senator and US congressman.

Still, Peggy was unlucky with her children, losing them all at very young ages save her son Stephen Jr., the third to bear that name. Peggy died afflicted by gout and probably stomach cancer at a young age—only 42. Hamilton, in fact, was with Peggy when she died. He sent a somber note to his wife that stated: "On Saturday, my dear Eliza, your sister took leave of her sufferings and friends, I trust to find repose and happiness in a better country."

"It was a cruel stroke, and made a profound impression among the large circle of kinspeople up and down the Hudson. The pomp and circumstance of her funeral at the manor house, with the retinue of tenants in mourning and their subsequent entertainment, is among the traditions of Albany" (Humphreys 239). She was initially buried in the family plot at the Van Rensselaer estate, and later reinterred at Albany Rural Cemetery. Meanwhile Hamilton's championing her husband's candidacy for New York governor after her death was one of several elements that provoked Hamilton's duel with Burr.

Jasmine Cephas Jones originated the roles of Maria Reynolds and Peggy Schuyler Off-Broadway, and she took them to Broadway as well. In 2016, Jones won a Grammy Award for her work as one of the principal soloists on the Hamilton cast album. Her spunkiness and shyness as Peggy, contrasted with bad girl Maria, make her a memorable part of the cast.

MARIA REYNOLDS

"Alexander's reputation flew so high in some camps that in other camps people wished for his complete destruction. In the newspapers, in private letters and gossip, wild assertions about his illegitimacy, dubious parentage, immigrant status, aristocratic tendencies, secret allegiance to the crown, and, increasingly, infidelities and sexual perversions swirled around him," Mazzeo reports (125). This was one of several factors that led to his political downfall one hot, sticky Philadelphia summer.

> Yellow fever broke out. But Alexander would not go. Government business consumed him. The work in the Treasury was too compelling, too important, and if Alexander would not go, neither would Eliza. She was determined for them not to be apart as a family: Too many times an absence of weeks turned into months, and Eliza hated the idea of being stuck alone again without Alexander in Albany. It brought back memories of the earliest years of their marriage. Memories came to her of waiting at the wharf and quarreling about letters. While they stalled, the health of both suffered. Finally, during the first week of September, Alexander gave in to General Schuyler's demands and the dictates of reason and accepted that the city was simply too unsafe for the children. Eliza, he explained to her gently, would have to go up to Albany at least until the cold weather came in at the end of October. He was her husband, and those were his wishes, he asked her obedience in this matter, and, by law and by custom, Eliza had no choice as a wife but to give it. (Mazzeo 145)

HAMILTON'S WOMEN

Born Mary Lewis but going by the more artistic Maria, Mrs. Reynolds is the story's femme fatale. In fact, in the show, she's more effective than Jefferson at destroying Hamilton…by undermining him with lust and his own arrogance rather than a straightforward battle. "Even though all of the other men—Jefferson, Lafayette, Mulligan, and of course, Burr—hate him personally and politically, they can't get rid of him until they follow the money trail of his affair," Wolf explains. Of course, her character is shaped as the classic "bad girl," complete with slippery song and bright red dress. Recasting her from shy Peggy also emphasizes their dichotomy as good girl/bad girl. She seduces Hamilton in a thick blues number. Of course, like Angelica and Eliza, Maria only exists and functions in the musical in relation to him—she seduces him and thus ruins his reputation forever.

While this episode in the musical is really about Hamilton, feminist historian Catherine Allgor sees the scene as one of the show's few reminders of the brutal sexism of the time: "Understanding that married women were completely dependent on their husbands, and consequently completely vulnerable if a spouse did not live up to the patriarchal bargain, explains Maria Reynolds's desperation, Alexander's response, and the implications of their extramarital affair" (107). She has only one commodity to trade—her body—so she does.

Maria was a child-bride, married at 15 and a mother by 17. She passed into her husband's control, allowing him to spend all their money and leave her destitute. In fact, the laws of coverture, insisting that James Reynolds had complete financial control over his wife and her dowry, also gave his anger a new path foreign to modern viewers' experience: "Alexander did not just 'cheat' with his wife but also stole from him. As the husband and wife were one, their affair was an assault on James in a way, as well as on the social order. James has earned the right not only to be angry but also to be righteous and to extract a profit from the situation," Allgor explains (107).

She greets Alexander in the song "Say No to This" with a

plea for assistance. "My husband's doing me wrong, beating me, cheating me, mistreating me. Suddenly he's up and gone. I don't have the means to go on," she tells him. He was indeed brutal. "[She] told me, so infamous was the Perfidy of Reynolds, that he had frequently enjoined and insisted that she should insinuate herself on certain high and influential Characters,—endeavour to make Assignations with them, and actually prostitute herself to gull Money from them."— her former landlord, Richard Falwell, explained.

"With a seeming air of affliction she [Maria] informed that she was a daughter of a Mr. Lewis, sister to a Mr. G. Livingston of the State of New-York, and wife to a Mr. Reynolds whose father was in the Commissary Department during the war with Great Britain, that her husband, who for a long time had treated her very cruelly, had lately left her, to live with another woman, and in so destitute a condition..." Hamilton writes in the Reynolds Pamphlet. After her husband had deserted her and his creditors in New York, she came seeking him, dependent on him as she was. There were no other options: If she had gotten a job or even had prostituted herself, all the money would have gone to her husband. Hamilton goes on to explain that Maria approached him by establishing her social credentials and then explained her terrible misfortunes and requested a loan so she could leave her cruel husband and return to her family.

> Her husband had left her for another woman, and she hoped that Hamilton, as a fellow New Yorker, would give her enough money to get back to the Empire State and sympathetic relatives. This, it should be emphasized, is Hamilton's version of the story. Hamilton said he did not have much cash in his house (an oddity in itself) but would be glad to lend her the money later in the day. Maria gave him her address, 134 South Fourth Street, only a block away from Hamilton's Third Street home, and departed. That evening, Hamilton put a thirty-dollar bank bill in his pocket and strolled to the Reynolds house. It was as expensive and comfortably furnished as the one Hamilton was renting—a fact that should have aroused his suspicions. A servant led him upstairs to Maria Reynolds's bedroom, where she greeted him with effusive gratitude and accepted the money. They talked for

HAMILTON'S WOMEN

> a while and, as Hamilton later described it, he became aware
> that "other than pecuniary consolation would be acceptable.
> (Fleming 230)

She sought help from a distant relative—basically her only option in her circumstances. Considering that she visited Hamilton's house in broad daylight while his wife was home, it seems likely that she was seeking honorable assistance. On hearing her request, Alexander promised her money the next day, asked her address, and brought it to her home. She agreed to sleep with him there, or perhaps offered. Hamilton reports that her forward behavior startled him. However, considering that he had brought money to her room, it seems at least suggestive that this woman who had been forced to prostitute herself before felt an obligation to repay his kindness.

In his own account of this story in the Reynolds Pamphlet, Hamilton describes soon getting suspicious that she had seduced him to compromise him, but he continued to see Maria as "her conduct made it extremely difficult to disentangle myself" (Villegas 246). As he adds, "All the appearances of violent attachment and of agonizing distress at the idea of a relinquishment, were played off with a most imposing art" (Villegas 246). Chernow gives his own commentary, deciding: "There seems little question that she approached Hamilton as part of an extortion racket, delivering an adept performance as a despairing woman. It was also clear, however, that she was too flighty to stick to any script (366-367). Hamilton also admits that her artificial hysterics may have duped him into vanity at thinking she was sincere: "My sensibility, perhaps my vanity, admitted the possibility of a real fondness" (Villegas 246). The show takes a similar angle, though showing her as unaware of her husband's schemes. "I didn't know any better!" she insists. Both are victims of Mr. Reynolds' opportunism.

> Hamilton is intellectually sharp and politically determined, able
> to withstand every pressure except the sexual appeal of a woman. His downfall is his weakness for a woman's seductive power,
> the weakness of sexual desire, which the musical portrays as un-

81

> derstandable: he's alone in the city; he's exhausted; he knows he should "say no to this." We feel bad that he couldn't resist her. The music is irresistible to the audience, as we witness her pressing him, professing her desire and her need, her helplessness. As *The New Yorker*'s Schulman writes, "While the show doesn't let Hamilton off the hook, he comes across more as a dupe than as an adulterer." But then, the show doesn't even give Maria the power of a villain, as she is ultimately the pawn in her husband's blackmail scheme. (Wolf)

The show emphasizes that Hamilton is stressed out and missing his wife, needing some kind of outlet in his personal life. Confronted with the request from Eliza and Angelica to come upstate, which he turns down, he likely feels guilty as well. As Hamilton considers Maria's proposition, ghostly chorus figures dance around them, protesting his decision like his conscience and suggesting the lost, adulterous figures of his childhood who stained his reputation forever. The lights swirl like a whirlpool sucking him down. Nonetheless, he succumbs.

Maria, his new romance, appears as a foil to his sanctioned romance with Eliza: "Hamilton raps and Maria sings her part in R&B—this gives them classic gender roles but also parallels his courtship of Eliza, giving it something of an unwholesome reprise" (Frankel). In her bright bad-girl crimson, she contrasts the green that Hamilton and his wife wear in much of Act II. She sobs and pleads, even describing herself as "helpless" like Eliza.

Still, the "bad girl" is responsible for seducing him as she pleads for him to stay. "Though the musical focuses on this misstep and his naiveté in believing that confessing the affair keeps him politically clean, this major plot device—Hamilton's destruction —is caused by a woman. Again, this narrative is far too culturally familiar" (Wolf). Women are cast as evil seductresses and Hamilton as mostly unable to resist despite his education and moral system. Like Hamilton, Fleming (in his book on the First Fathers' biggest scandals) sees Maria as the manipulator of events:

HAMILTON'S WOMEN

> In all these encounters, Maria, proved herself a consummate actress. She portrayed herself as a once naive woman who had married the scoundrel Reynolds at the age of fifteen, had a child by him, and found herself trapped in an ongoing nightmare. He turned her into a prostitute who handed over all the money she received from her clients so he could gamble in the stock market. This victimized version of Maria's marriage [was false]—she actually seems to have been closer to a partner in crime. (Fleming 232)

Why did such an intelligent hero succumb to her trickery, and why did such a loving husband stray? His own account is a bit vague on this point, though both questions certainly can be answered by the expected gender roles of the time. Hamilton's own sensitivity may also have contributed, according to Fleming:

> Did pity play a part in Hamilton's seduction? Did Maria remind him of his mother's travails with an angry husband and several lovers? Why didn't the secretary of the treasury consider that he, the most powerful man in Philadelphia, except for President George Washington, might be the target of a plot to ruin his reputation? Was he so deep in his romance with fame that he considered himself invulnerable? Was Maria Reynolds a kind of damaged version of Angelica Church—a woman who made no secret of her attraction to men and her awareness that men desired her? That may be the best answer to Hamilton's readiness to offer Maria "consolation"—a significant choice of words. (230)

When Reynolds finds out about the affair, he demands money ($1,000 or the equivalent of nearly $25,000 today) to keep quiet and offers in return to not tell Hamilton's wife but also allows him to keep seeing Maria, playing simultaneously on his fear of discovery and his lust. Meanwhile, Maria pleads her ignorance and begs Hamilton to not leave her. This scene in the show emphasizes her lack of options—her husband owns her financially and legally and she can only entreat Hamilton to keep their relationship going. With this, her character exemplifies the rigid gender roles of the time.

Though what Hamilton did was wrong, the musical does its best to excuse him and certainly to show his frame of mind in "Say No to This" (in which, as the title emphasizes, he tries to refuse but his lust is too much for him) and "Hur-

83

ricane" in which he makes a desperate gesture to try to save himself but destroys himself instead.

> The musical offers these power dynamics—both diegetically and performatively—in a nuanced and complex way. Because the show is told from Hamilton's point of view, even though the other men hate him, the musical sides with him. He's charming and likeable and politically brave. Though he talks too much and "writes like he's running out of time," he's passionate and opinionated and fully committed to the creation of this new country. From a historical distance, then, he seems perfectly reasonable. He's ambitious and a workaholic but those traits seem appropriate and admirable given the high stakes of the moment. He's more sympathetic than the other men, partly because he has more stage time and he's a fully developed character. (Wolf)

Historically, when Hamilton's accusers (congressmen James Monroe, Abraham Venable, and Fredrick Muhlenberg) came calling, he showed them the letters the Reynolds had sent him. The accusers speedily turned from accusatory to apologetic, apologizing for prying. In the society of the time, among gentlemen, it was considered incredibly inappropriate to discuss such personal matters. The scandal, Hamilton hoped, was settled, as he offered more and more letters, oversharing details of his personal life. However, James Monroe kept some, insisting that they might be necessary to clear the government of scandal, though as a gentleman, he would never release them.

In 1979, Republican journalist and gossipmonger James T. Callender published a series of pamphlets titled *The History of the United States for 1796*. In them, he insisted Hamilton had not only had an affair with Maria but had speculated unlawfully with her husband James and laundered money through him. The letters, presumably handed from Monroe to his close friend Jefferson, who had given them to Callender, were released at last.

> Callender did not care much about Hamilton's sexual escapades. Indeed, he was skeptical of the story that Hamilton had told the congressmen about having had an affair with Maria Reynolds, even believing that the treasury secretary had forged her supposed letters. Instead, Callender was persuaded that Hamilton,

HAMILTON'S WOMEN

> privy to insider information, had used Treasury Department funds to speculate in government securities. He had, to use today's terminology, laundered the money through James Reynolds. To Callender's way of thinking, Hamilton's yarn about paying blackmail was a smokescreen to mask his improper conduct at the Treasury. (Bloomsbury 292)

Hamilton, fearing his financial system would be undermined by these charges, published the Reynolds Pamphlet, readily confessing to the affair, and in fact, oversharing once more, in an effort to clear his name of the financial crime. At once, Hamilton understood that Callender's publication threatened him with enormous personal and political damage, harming his chances of political office in future. He yearned to clear his name. "Consumed with the need for respect, Hamilton feared being seen as not only 'unprincipled but a fool'," Bloomsbury explains (292). In his writing, Hamilton insisted that this is the most heinous attack on him of all the many in his political career.

He likewise acknowledged the pain he will be causing his wife with the public confession, but added, "That bosom will approve, that even at so great an expense I should effectively wipe away a more serious stain from a name which it cherishes with no less elevation than tenderness" (Villegas 242). In other words, Eliza would support his choice because his clearing his name mattered to her too. Here, Hamilton acknowledged his family's pain but prioritized his own reputation above it, naively deciding that his wife would agree.

With his publication, Hamilton sought to show that he was so honest and public about his infidelity that there was no way he had stolen from the treasury. However, he miscalculated. In fact, the American people were scandalized by his brazen immorality.

> It was a sordid, and salacious, confession, and he begged for forgiveness, crying out: "I can never cease to condemn myself." But in all of American political history, perhaps no figure ever acted as unwisely as did Hamilton in coming clean. His was a tale of having been a slave to passion, a disclosure of having been bamboozled by a couple of unsavory con artists, and a shocking admission that he had persisted in sleeping with Maria even after

> her husband was aware of what was occurring. Friends stuck by him, but many others greeted his avowal with ridicule. Callender gushed ecstatically that Hamilton's admission was "worth all that fifty of the best pens in America could have said against him." In no time, Hamilton was spoofed in a New York theatrical production. Many thought the revelations raised troubling questions about his character and judgment. (Bloomsbury 293)

In a strange twist, Burr was actually Maria's divorce lawyer, and then the ward for her daughter, who was fostered elsewhere to avoid being embroiled in the scandal (Isenberg 121). He assisted many orphans and wards in cases such as this, though his motive for getting tangled in Hamilton's affair was less clear.

Of course, there are other possibilities to be seen in this sordid tale. In her biography of Eliza Hamilton, Mazzeo boldly suggests a revision to history (and indeed the beliefs of the musical), suggesting that there was no sex scandal. She believes Jefferson and his friends' guess was correct—that Hamilton was involved in speculation and money-laundering through his distant relative James Reynolds, and that he had forged the love letters from Maria—which she fervently denied writing—to save himself from ruin and political scandal. Further, Mazzeo believes Eliza gave her consent for the scheme, to preserve her family.

> First was the question of why Alexander would not release the handwritten documents he claimed were in his possession. "If the letters published by Mr. Hamilton in the name of Maria are genuine," James Callender opined, "it would be very easy to obtain her testation of the fact." And if—as Callender knew she would—Maria Reynolds claimed they were fabrications, why would Alexander not introduce the letters and agree to allowing a judge to make a handwriting comparison? Maria Reynolds was quite willing. Second, Callender drew the public attention to the many internal insistencies in the transcriptions Alexander had published in the pamphlet. "These letters from Mrs. Reynolds," Callender noted. are badly spelt and pointed. Capitals, also, occur even in the midst of words. But waving such excrescences, the stile is pathetic [i.e., moving] and even elegant. It does not bear the marks of an illiterate writer. The construction of the periods disagrees with this apparent incapacity of spelling.... A few

HAMILTON'S WOMEN

> gross blunders are interspersed, and these could readily be devised; but, when stript of such a veil, the body of the composition is pure and correct....The whole collection would not have required above an evening to write.... You speak as if it was impossible to invent a few letters. (101)

Some mysteries, of course, will never be solved. Publicly, Eliza stood by him (however she felt privately). George Washington also offered public support, sending a gift of a silver wine cooler. While the attached card didn't mention the affair, it emphasized that Washington still considered himself Hamilton's "sincere friend," and the timing suggests that Washington wanted to show his friendship to the country when Hamilton most needed it (Villegas 251). America, of course, filled with gossip, to the point at which the Philadelphia *Aurora* joked that the new national library should include "*The Cuckold's Chronicle* for the use of General Hamilton."

James T. Callender, the man who had published the Reynolds letters, received no reward from Jefferson or his administration. He followed this by publicizing that Jefferson had put him up to it, and then launched a fresh sex scandal. He revealed that President Jefferson had fathered half a dozen children with Sally Hemings, the half-sister of his late wife. Even as he moved from scandal to scandal, the disaster of this one never left Hamilton.

VALERIE ESTELLE FRANKEL

PART II:
THE UNSEEN WOMEN

VALERIE ESTELLE FRANKEL

MRS. BURR

Burr's father, Aaron Burr, Senior, was president of the College of New Jersey (now Princeton College) and a powerful preacher. His mother, Esther Edwards Burr, he calls a "genius" in "Wait For It." Indeed, she was the daughter of Reverend John Edwards and a very independent spirit. One contemporary spoke of her "unaffected, natural freedom," and said, likely inspiring the musical's line, that "her genius was more than common" (Isenberg 4). She was named for her great-grandmother Esther Stoddard, who was a woman of great spiritual authority, leading women's prayer groups and winning a reputation for being even more forceful and learned than her distinguished husband. Esther Edwards underwent conversion as a teenager, and in 1752 she followed the path of her great-grandmother and mother when she married a minister, Aaron Burr, sixteen years her senior, self-assured, and personally appealing. Their children Sarah ("Sally") and Aaron Jr. were born in Newark in 1754 and 1756.

From 1754 through 1757, Esther Edwards Burr wrote a daily letter-journal to her friend Sarah Prince, one of the earliest extensive accounts of a colonial American woman's daily life. She interpreted every aspect of her life through the primary cultural institution there, the Puritan evangelical church. This 300-page journal, filled with witty comments on literature, politics, and religion, as well as a record of her public defense of women, has survived (Isenberg 4). It puts Puritan beliefs in context, showing how women of the time lived and saw the world through their faith. The journal describes visitations to the sick, attendance at sermons, entertainment of the governor's wife with "cakes" on militia day, the destruction of the French and Indian War, the political maneuverings of the Newark community, and the difficulties of moving to Princeton and establishing the college—all combined with frank, moral assessments of what Mrs. Burr thinks of her neighbors. Her commentary on the protestations of the local government as it prepared to meet upcoming battle is typical:

I am perplexed about our publick affairs, the Men say (tho not Mr. Burr, he is not of that sort) that women have no business to concern themselves about 'em but to trust to those that know better and be content to be destroyed—because they did all for the best—Indeed, if I was convinced that our great men did as they really thought was for the Glory of God and the good of the country, it would go a great ways to make me easy. ("Esther Edwards Burr")

Though she died when her son Aaron was very young, he grew up with her legacy.

Aaron Burr, Senior, died of illness in 1757, and Esther in 1758, in the same illness that took her own father. Sarah Edwards, Esther's mother, came to take charge of the children and she soon died too. In just over a year, the Burr children had lost both parents, two grandparents, and also a great-grandfather. Burr was only two when these tragedies occurred. "Though he lacked any memory of these gruesome events, Burr was even more emphatically orphaned than Hamilton," Chernow reports (191).

In this isolation, Aaron was very close with his sister, two years older, to whom he wrote frequently. "She had been his one female confidante, the trusted recipient of his journalistic musings on sex and polite society as he was coming of age," his biographer writes (Isenberg 69). They were passed between relatives and family friends until they came of age.

THEODOSIA I AND HER MARK ON HISTORY

Miranda describes Theodosia as his way into Burr's character: "He waited until she was available...imagine Hamilton waiting—for anything" (Miranda 86). Theodosia Bartow Prevost (November 1746—May 18, 1794), married a British Army officer, Jacques Marcus Prevost, at age seventeen. They had five children, who remained with her in New Jersey, while her husband was stationed in the West Indies. Meanwhile, Theodosia, her mother, and younger half-sister, faced survival amidst guerilla warfare in heavily contested Bergen County from late 1776 into the early 1780s.

Though her husband and also her stepfather were British officers, Theodosia aligned herself with the Revolution. She even successfully played both sides, convincing the British military (and her husband!) that she was a devoted wife, even while hosting the patriots. "Tutored at home, she had been exposed to a cosmopolitan education that was unusual among colonial Americans" (Isenberg 65). Stories of her include making up poems on the spot and conversing about the great writings of the time in polished French. Theodosia's home, the Hermitage—named after the cottage of Jean-Jacques Rousseau—was a sort of French salon of wit and learning, and soon became a gathering-place for American soldiers. At her invitation, Washington made this place his headquarters after the Battle of Monmouth. Like many women, she made herself invaluable to the Revolution. She spied for them, using ladies' gossip to elicit many important confidences. In turn, the men protected her property instead of confiscating

VALERIE ESTELLE FRANKEL

it, and treated her gallantly. In their eyes she was a "chaste republican matron," an older woman worthy of their esteem (Isenberg 66).

> Reinventing chivalry, Continental officers fostered what can best be described as a romantic cult of republican matrons. The language they used derived from the medieval model of courtly love, and encouraged devotion to mature women. The difference in age and status implied a relationship that existed on a higher, more spiritual plane, and which made the younger man's admiration appear noble and altruistic...For Whigs Monroe, Troup, and Burr, chastened lust rose from beneath the surface of this new, revivified version of courtly love. (Isenberg 68)

Theodosia first met Aaron Burr in August 1778 on a five-day sail to New York. The two struck up a friendship, and Burr began visiting her regularly. At first, he was one courtly admirer of many, though things slowly changed.

> He encounters Theodosia while protecting her home from American raiders who impute the Toryism of the deceased to his widow. She admires the dark-eyed, black-haired young officer, a common reaction among Burr's female acquaintances. Less predictable is the affection develops toward *her*. She is ten years his elder and neither beautiful nor rich. But she *is* intelligent, educated and willing to speak her mind. The women Burr grew up among were sometimes intelligent and often outspoken, but none had much education or seemed to miss it; Burr is fascinated by this woman with whom he can converse as an equal. (Brands 6)

Indeed, he told her in his letters that, "It was knowledge of your mind that first impressed me with respect for that of your sex" (Isenberg 81). Despite a 10-year age gap, they became lovers, and when Theodosia discovered her husband had died of yellow fever in 1781, the pair were free to marry. He wrote to his sister in November 1778, "Believe me, Sally, she has an honest and affectionate heart. We talk of you very often, her highest happiness will be to see you and love you" (Isenberg 69). Among the Founding Mothers, she stands apart for her sparkling intellect and devotion to education: "Neither Hamilton nor Jefferson married a woman who evidenced such force of character and independence of view" (Kennedy 60).

HAMILTON'S WOMEN

Burr and Theodosia modeled their relationship on the eighteenth century's ideal of an intellectual friendship—a model actually meant to be shared between men. In keeping with his fascination for Theodosia, Burr was quite feminist, admiring Mary Wollstonecraft's groundbreaking *The Vindication of the Rights of Women,* in which she stressed the need for women to develop their minds through education. "That ultra-liberal 1792 work rocked British and American society; but Burr had already begun practicing its egalitarian marital principles ten years before its publication," Isenberg writes (72). He wrote to Theodosia recommending it and the pair continued to model its ideals.

Further, Theodosia had her own small mark on history— one more that made the history books but not the show. Shortly before Angelica's own marriage, Peggy Shippen threw over handsome captured British Major John André to wed Major Benedict Arnold. "What no one at Morristown knew yet was that Peggy Arnold was already an enemy informant and an agent for the British spymaster John André. Within months, she would bring her disgruntled husband into the network, culminating in a stunning betrayal" (Mazzeo 65). When Benedict Arnold betrayed the American forces, Hamilton pursued him. He found his wife, Peggy, who prevailed on Hamilton's chivalry. She raved like a madwoman, insisting the spirits had taken her husband. "In an era when men used the term 'hysteria' to marginalize women and when women displayed various forms of 'hysteria' in desperate bids for empowerment, Peggy reacted to amazing events in an astonishing way. She suddenly, inexplicably, and loudly behaved as if she had lost her mind" (Jacob and Case 160).

Peggy asked the housekeeper to see how Arnold's senior aide, Lieutenant Colonel Richard Varick, was feeling, and "no sooner had the housekeeper turned her back" than Peggy ran after her, shouting in a bizarre fashion." Varick heard shrieks and got up from his bed. He said he found Peggy in great distress, "with her hair disheveled and flowing around her neck; her morning gown with no other clothes remained on her, too few to be seen even by a gentleman of the family, much less by many strangers" (Jacob and Case 160-161). She claimed not to recognize Washington and shrieked that they all intended to kill her baby.

> While Hamilton was no master of psychology, he was adept at publicity. His letter to his friend John Laurens about Arnold's treachery was published in American newspapers, increasing Hamilton's fame while providing a prominent defense for Peggy. "It was impossible not to have been touched with her situation," Hamilton wrote. "Everything affecting in female tears, or in the misfortunes of beauty; everything pathetic in the wounded tenderness of a wife, or in the apprehensive fondness of a mother; and, till I have reason to change the opinion, I will add, everything amiable in suffering innocence conspired to make her an object of sympathy to all who were present." Even in a letter to Elizabeth Schuyler, the woman he would marry in a few months, Hamilton seemed a bit too interested in Mrs. Arnold. "She received us in bed with every circumstance that would interest our sympathy," Hamilton wrote. "Her sufferings were so eloquent that I wished myself her brother to have a right to become her defender. (Jacob and Case 166)

Hamilton was fooled and sent her home to her father. However, she stopped at the Hermitage in New Jersey, where Theodosia Prevost lived. According to some accounts, she confessed everything to her—not knowing her loyalties were compromised. The two women apparently had much in common, inspiring Peggy's trust:

> Like Peggy, Prevost was a fifth-generation American born to privilege. The well-read Prevost spoke fluent French and proved herself the intellectual equal of the prominent men who surrounded her. Like Peggy, she had married young. At age seventeen, Prevost wed a Swiss born lieutenant colonel serving in the British army in farflung locations such as the southern states and the Caribbean. Like Peggy, she achieved social standing with officers on both sides of the war. While married to a man loyal to the crown, she made close friends with champions of independence, such as James Madison, who would become president, and Aaron Burr, who would become both vice president and her husband. And like Peggy, Prevost was a survivor. Madison praised her "gaiety in the midst of affliction.'" By the time Peggy stopped at Hermitage in late September 1780, Prevost probably had

HAMILTON'S WOMEN

> started her love affair with Burr, though her marriage wouldn't
> end until the next year, when her husband died of yellow fever
> in Jamaica. (Jacob and Case 170)

Burr's memoirs report that Peggy felt comfortable enough with Theodosia to unburden herself, to admit that she had been putting on a show. "As soon as they were left alone, Mrs. Arnold became tranquilized, and assured Mrs. Prevost that she was heartily sick of the theatrics she was exhibiting," Burr recalled. "She stated that she had corresponded with the British commander—that she was disgusted with the American cause and those who had the management of public affairs—and that, through great persuasion and unceasing perseverance, she had ultimately brought the general into an arrangement to surrender West Point to the British" (Jacob and Case 170). Thus Theodosia unraveled Peggy Arnold's treachery and presence of innocence that had so fooled Hamilton and the Founding Fathers and reported it to Washington and his staff.

By November 1778, Aaron Burr's constant visits to the Hermitage provoked gossip, with Paterson baldly referring to Theodosia as "the object of [Burr's] Affections" (Isenberg 69). As a proponent of education and self-empowerment, she encouraged him to pass the bar and find a means of income, which he did just before their marriage.

They married on July 2, 1782 at the Hermitage. Their first child, and the only one to survive to adulthood, was born on June 21, 1783, and also named Theodosia. After her, two boys were stillborn, and daughter Sally Burr (named for Aaron's sister) died at age three. The family moved to New York in 1783, echoing the scene in the musical in which Burr sings to his young daughter, as Hamilton's neighbor and competitor in law. As Burr entered politics, Theodosia's keen sense of observation and adeptness at judging Burr's peers on the national scene made her a crucial ally, particularly after he joined the United States Senate in 1791.

> While she lived, Theodosia Burr endorsed and enlarged her husband's predisposition to accept women as peers—the Edwards
> women were formidable as well—and led him to organize his

VALERIE ESTELLE FRANKEL

> feelings into a protofeminist position on female education. That, in turn, brought them to propose a role for women in government that was novel even in New Jersey, where women voted in 1790. Unlike Jefferson's and Hamilton's, Burr's character was molded by the love of a woman of immense force and intelligence. Theodosia drew forth from him all that was most admirable; he had already been a heroic soldier, but she made of him an adventurer of the intellect. There were many military heroes in those times, but she asked more of Burr than physical courage and endurance. To satisfy her, he must set forth into unknown emotional territory amid the tempests of feeling between men and women, venturing where none other of the Founders dared go. (Kennedy 59)

Around 1792, Theodosia fell into a constant state of pain and eventually Burr took over the younger Theodosia's studies. His wife Theodosia died May 18, 1794 of stomach or uterine cancer, at age 48. Burr and Theo comforted each other; the experience bound the thirty-eight-year-old widower and the eleven-year-old girl more tightly than ever. Each was all the other had left of the one they had lost. "The mother of my Theo was the best woman and finest lady I have ever known," Burr sadly observed (Brands 22). She was buried in St. John's Burying Ground, which was associated with Trinity Church.

During *Hamilton*'s Off-Broadway run, the song "Let it Go" shows Hamilton confronting Burr in a more violent exchange over the stolen senate seat and Burr confiding in Eliza that his wife is feeling ill. Another cut scene, "Dear Theodosia" had a brief reprise, between "Burn" and "Blow Us All Away," in which Burr is telling his daughter that her mother has passed away.

> Dear Theodosia, how to say to you
> Sometime last night, your mother breathed your name
> And like a flame that flickers out too soon, she died
> She's gone

"Flickered out too soon" suggests that, in his grief, Burr feels he didn't have enough time with his wife. Certainly, their early romance was marred by Burr's "waiting" for her to be unattached, and now the sudden tragedy of her death has stunned him. Dissatisfaction with the time one has in life is a recurring theme in this show. Miranda has said this reprise was cut from the Broadway version because it dedicated too much time to two off-stage characters. Further, Burr's wife and daughter both having the same name was somewhat confusing to the audience. These cuts, of course, allow the story to focus more on Hamilton's own life.

Burr's sister Sarah (Sally) did not long outlive her, subjecting Burr to a double blow. She had married Tapping Reeve, their old tutor, on June 24, 1772 at age eighteen. Reeve made his mark on history by opening the Litchfield Law School, one of the earliest law schools in the United States. Their home, now known as Tapping Reeve House and Law School, was designated a National Historic Landmark in 1965. On October 3, 1780 she gave birth to their only child, Aaron Burr Reeve (1780-1809), though he and his own son both died young. Sally died in 1797 at age 43, after being in poor health throughout much of her adult life. She and her brother had been close and he poignantly grieved her loss.

THEODOSIA II

The cut scene in the song "Schuyler Defeated" discussed Young Theodosia's adulthood alongside her mother's illness:

ELIZA: And how's your daughter?
BURR: She's my pride and joy. Fluent in French and Latin!
PHILIP: So am I!
BURR: She's the same age as your boy.

This scene stresses how the two children have similar education and upbringings—unusual for the time. In fact, Burr's daughter Theodosia was actually quite a prodigy. He educated her as a boy, ensuring she could read and write by age three. Both Burr and his wife had a "passionate commitment to education," so Theodosia educated her daughter as any wealthy male child would have been: she had read *Decline and Fall of the Roman Empire* by age ten. She was taught Hebrew, Latin, Greek, Spanish, French, botany, natural history, geography, mathematics, and the classics of political theory with many hours of study daily. There were also riding, skating, and dancing.

Theo was brought up lovingly and idolized her father from the moment she could express herself. "She frequently talks of, and falls on, her dear papa," her mother wrote Burr when the child was two and he was away. "Your dear Theodosia cannot hear you, spoken of without an apparent melancholy; insomuch that her nurse is obliged to exert her invention to divert her, and myself avoid to mention you in her presence. She was one whole day indifferent to everything but your name, Her attachment is not of a common nature" (Brands 7).

The title and structure of "Dear Theodosia" suggests a letter, likely a reference to Burr and his daughter's spirited correspondence, still preserved. In it, Burr sings adoringly to his baby girl about the country he will build for her:

> You and I will build a strong foundation
> And I'll be here for you
> The way is clear for you to blow us all away

His wording emphasizes women's contributions behind the scenes at the time, and perhaps in their forefront as "The way is clear for you to blow us all away." He envisioned her as a prodigy and thus shaped her into one. Kennedy observes, "Burr's letters to his daughter Theodosia are not like either Jefferson's or Hamilton's. They graduate from straightforward instruction, when she was very young, to comradery, when she was beyond twelve or so, but they never patronize" (60). He also was indeed there for her as his song promises, devoting himself to her education before and after her marriage and corresponding with her constantly.

Having grown up an orphan, he was very aware of what the loss of a father could do to a child. Indeed, he never lacked time for her daughter. "Enclosed in Bartow's last letter came one which, from the handwriting, I supposed to be

HAMILTON'S WOMEN

from that great fat fellow. Colonel Troup," he wrote her not long before her tenth Christmas. "Judge of my pleasure and surprise when I opened and found it was from my dear little girl. You improve much in your writing. Let your next be in small hand." As he added, he hoped she would write soon, for Theo continued to write less often than her father desired. "Why do you neither acknowledge nor answer my last letter? That is not kind—it is scarcely civil. I beg you will not take a fortnight to answer this, as you did the other.... I love to hear from you, and still more to receive your letters," he added (Brands 14).

He had an idealistic image of her future as he did for America, and he pursued both as he blended them with his own interests. Burr's use of "you and I" emphasizes her destiny in building a nation beside and after him—not just a family. In fact, she was to wed into a very rich and influential plantation family in the South, with a political base that Burr hoped would make him president. Chernow notes, "Burr had always doted on his daughter Theodosia, playing a Pygmalion role as he molded her into his image of womanly perfection. In so doing, he converted her into one of America's most literate young women" (698). Burr wrote to his wife, "If I could foresee that Theo would become a *mere* fashionable woman, with all the attentive frivolity and vacuity of mind, adorned with whatever grace and allurement, I would earnestly pray God to take her forthwith hence" (Isenberg 80). Indeed, she became far more.

Burr wrote to his wife in 1793, echoing Wollstonecraft, "But I hope yet by her, to convince the world what neither sex appear to believe—that women have souls!" (Isenberg 81). True, he had no expectation that she would go into politics or law. "Yet he would have felt perfectly comfortable with her voting or holding political office. He was, by any definition, a feminist" (Isenberg 83).

> Burr credits his wife as well for his appreciation of women's abilities. "It was a knowledge of your mind which first inspired me with a respect for that of your sex," he writes the elder Theodo-

VALERIE ESTELLE FRANKEL

> sia. "And with some regret I confess that the ideas which you have often heard me express in favor of female intellectual powers are founded on what I have imagined, more than what I have seen, except in you." He ponders why others have not allowed women to advance. "I have endeavored to trace the causes of this *rare* display of genius in women, and find them in the errors of education, of prejudice, and of habit. I admit that men are equally, nay more, much more to blame than women. Boys and girls are generally educated much in the same way till they are eight or nine years of age, and it is admitted that girls make at least equal progress with the boys; generally, indeed, they make better. Why, then, has it never been thought worth the attempt to discover, by fair experiment, the particular age at which the male superiority becomes so evident. (Brands 16-17)

Isenberg observes, "He made her an apprentice and later confidante, instilling within her a mental firmness and ability to command respect" (82). These were traditional male qualities of the time, and he wanted to show her off to the world as the equal of a man. He proudly raised her as fathers of his time were raising boys, not girls and soon wrote to her as a peer. As she grew up, he wrote letters of his affairs, mocking his mistresses with rather disturbing frankness.

In 1800, Theodosia fell for a South Carolina planter. "My father laughs at my impatience to hear from you," Theodosia wrote teasingly during a separation (Meares). Still, she and Joseph Alston (eventually to become governor of South Carolina) may have been a politically-motivated match as much as a love match. Burr lacked funds to the point at which he feared he would lose their beloved Richmond Hill, and Alston was one of the richest men in the South. As such, he also had a great deal of untapped political influence, which Burr may have hoped to exploit.

On January 2, 1801, the Electoral College votes were counted from the fateful election of 1800, which Burr lost, automatically making him Vice President. On the evening of February 2, 1801, Theodosia married Alston. They honeymooned briefly at Richmond Hill, and then traveled to Washington, where they watched Aaron Burr inaugurated as Vice President on March 4, 1801. Joseph and Theodosia then con-

HAMILTON'S WOMEN

tinued south to The Oaks, Alston's ancestral home near Georgetown, South Carolina. Theodosia was mostly happy with her new family, though she found plantation life at The Oaks strange and foreign. Summers, the most miserable part of the year, she spent with her father up north. Her son, Aaron Burr Alston, was born in 1802.

After becoming Vice President, Burr "kept up his usual unflappable air" as Chernow says, writing to his daughter describing his love life in great detail (677). Likewise, on June 23rd, after writing Hamilton a letter committing to their duel, he celebrated Theodosia's birthday at his home at Richmond Hill in her absence, writing to tell her how the guests "laughed an hour and danced an hour and drank her health" (698). While he advised her on studying botany and chemistry and instructed her how to build a wonderful library, he did not specifically mention the duel or his possible death. He did leave an instruction list in case he didn't survive, telling her which slaves to sell and insisting she burn incriminating letters he had written to his mistresses. He also acknowledged his life and joy at having her as a confidante. As Burr wrote his daughter:

> I am indebted to you, my dearest Theodosia, for a very great portion of the happiness which I have enjoyed in this life. You have completely satisfied all that my heart and affections had hoped or even wished. With a little more perseverance, determination, and industry, you will obtain all that my ambition or vanity had fondly imagined. Let your son have occasion to be proud that he had a mother. Adieu. Adieu. A. Burr.

The show emphasizes that, as in history, onstage she is his primary motivation. As he insists, preparing to shoot Hamilton, "I had only one thought before the slaughter/ This man will not make an orphan of my daughter!" She was married at the time (a fact unmentioned in the show), but either way, losing her father's guidance and companionship would have been a terrible blow.

Of course, his duel with Hamilton condemned him as a murderer and criminal in the public's eyes. He fled Hamilton's home base of New York, hiding out in Washington

VALERIE ESTELLE FRANKEL

D.C. After serving out his term as Vice President, Aaron Burr headed west. to establish a new country comprised of Mexico and the western North American territory and appoint himself emperor, with Theodosia and her son succeeding him. He had the full support of his daughter and son-in-law, who supplied much-needed funds and traveled to help him. Theodosia wrote to her half-brother excitedly about "the new settlement which I am about to establish" (Meares). However, the plot was discovered, and Burr was taken into custody.

The family closeness continued: When Aaron Burr was tried for treason in August 1807, Theodosia and her family loyally attended the trial, where he was finally exonerated for lack of proof. With his reputation in shreds, Burr slipped from New York to England, bidding Theo a touching goodbye first. He wrote to her from London of how eager everyone was to entertain him. However, depression, loneliness, and illness began taking her over in her plantation home. Alarmed by Theo's illness, Burr arranged to have her come visit in London, where he hoped local physicians could help her, but she was too ill, and tension between the countries was making travel unsafe.

Theo's health—she was probably in the final stages of uterine cancer—deteriorated further. "The most violent affections have tormented her during the whole of the last 18 months," she wrote in third-person to a doctor in 1808. "Hysteric fits, various colors and flashes of light before her yes, figures passing around her bed, strange noises, low spirits and worse." She missed her father intensely. "What indeed," she wrote him, "would I not risk once more to see him, to hang upon him, to place my child upon his knee, and again spend my days in the happy occupation of endeavoring to anticipate his wishes" (Meares).

In 1812, her sole child Aaron Burr Alton, age eleven, died of a sudden bout of malaria. Devastated, Theodosia wrote to her father, "There is no more joy for me, the world is blank. I have lost my boy, my child is gone forever" (Isenberg 387). A letter from Joseph Alston adds. "One dreadful blow has de-

104

HAMILTON'S WOMEN

stroyed us; reduced us to the veriest, most sublimated wretchedness. That boy, on whom all rested; our companion, our friend—he who was to have transmitted down the mingled blood of Theodosia and myself—he who was to have redeemed all your glory, and shed new lustre upon our families—that boy, at once our happiness and our pride, is taken from us—is dead." (Brands 162). Further, Theodosia was still critically ill herself. Alston, worried about her health, sent her to spend time with her father for a change of scene.

However, her ship was lost off North Carolina, with her final fate a mystery. "With her to the depths went all those documents which her father had hoped she might use to compose proper biographies of her mother, her father, and herself" (Kennedy 62). Poetically, she failed to preserve the family legacy like Eliza did her own. Burr had lost his great love and confidante in a single night. One might say that she, like her tragic counterpart Philip Hamilton, was quite literally "blown away" at sea. In the end, both young people, in whom their fathers had placed so many hopes, were lost—though Burr had no other family then.

Eventually, Burr had more marriages and several illegitimate children, but his legacy, as he thought, died with his grandson and daughter. Her final fate was never discovered.

> Many believed the *Patriot* had been captured by one of the pirate ships known to troll the Outer Banks. Over the years, numerous "death-bed confessions" from various aged or imprisoned pirates were reported in papers all over the country. The first to gain traction was the case of Jean DeFarges and Robert Johnson, who were executed in 1819 for other crimes. An 1820 article in the *New York Advertiser* claimed that the two had confessed to having been crew on the *Patriot*. They claimed to have led a mutiny, and scuttled the ship, killing all on board. In 1833, *The Mobile Commercial Register* reported that another man had confessed to raiding the *Patriot* with other pirates, who had reluctantly forced Theodosia to walk the plank. Other stories claimed that she had become the wife of an American Indian in Texas, been taken as a pirate's mistress to Bermuda, or that she had killed herself after resisting the advances of the pirate Octave Chauvet. Yet another fanciful story had her writing farewell

VALERIE ESTELLE FRANKEL

> letters to her father and husband, and stuffing them and her wedding ring into a champagne bottle and throwing it into the Carolina sea before being executed. (Meares)

Theodosia's tragic legend lived on for some time. Many novels, poems, and magazine articles resulted, with Robert Frost's "Kitty Hawk" noting, "Did I recollect how the wreckers wrecked Theodosia Burr off this very shore? / T'was to punish her, but her father more." Her ghost is said to haunt The Oaks, where her spirit is said to be chased by three headless pirates. Even as the public embraced the romantic possibilities, this mystery was never solved.

SALLY HEMINGS

One named character in the show actually was Black historically (beyond the rumors of Hamilton's own pedigree). Sally Hemings, asked to open Jefferson's mail on his return in "What Did I Miss?" was most likely his mistress and mother of his children, as well as the focus of Jefferson's great political sex scandal.

Sally Hemings had escorted Jefferson's daughter Polly to join him in Paris and stayed with the family thereafter for twenty-six months. Admittedly, there's little historical evidence of an affair. In 1873, Sally's son Madison told a newspaper interviewer that his mother had assured him that Jefferson was his father and that she had been his "concubine" in Paris (Adams 221). Further, she had apparently only been willing to return with him to Virginia on the assurance that her children would be freed at age twenty-one, an event that occurred on schedule.

"One of the stories that Angelica shared with Alexander privately was the scandalous account of the private life of her new continental friend, Thomas Jefferson, whose dalliance in Paris with Sally Hemings, a fair-skinned African slave from his plantation, had resulted already in mixed-race children.

HAMILTON'S WOMEN

Alexander tucked that story away in his memory" (Mazzeo 127). During Jefferson's presidential campaign of 1796 against John Adams, Hamilton came out swinging against Jefferson and unwisely dropped hints that the candidate's public veneer of "simplicity and humility afford but a flimsy veil to the internal evidences of aristocratic splendor, sensuality, and epicureanism," this last insult a veiled reference to Jefferson's sexual relationship in Paris (Mazzeo 127). However, since James Monroe had kept documents on the Reynolds affair, he released them in retaliation for the attack on Jefferson. When James Callender destroyed Hamilton's name through this but received no particular reward, he brought up Jefferson's own scandal.

> It was "well known" among Jefferson's neighbors that he had kept Sally "as his concubine" for many years, Callender declared. One of their children was a boy of about twelve named "Tom," with red hair and a striking resemblance to Jefferson. Supposedly, Tom had been conceived in Paris, when Sally escorted Maria Jefferson across the Atlantic to join her father. Everyone in the vicinity of Monticello knew about Sally. So did James Madison, when he urged Americans to vote for Jefferson because of his "virtue." Federalist editors leaped on the Sally story and gleefully reprinted it in their newspapers throughout the nation. As the Federalists saw it, they were retaliating against the Jeffersonian Republican editors who had revived the British slanders about Washington's supposed sexual sins in the Revolution and exposed Alexander Hamilton's affair with Maria Reynolds. (Fleming 310)

This second sex scandal also rocked the nation. Jefferson, however, had learned from Hamilton's disgrace. Even as he was shocked at James Callender's assaults on his personal character, his friends, such as James Madison, publically came to his defense with scathing denials even as they denounced Callender. Nonetheless, Jefferson declined to answer the charges publicly.

Beyond Sally, slavery gets a few mentions in the musical, emphasizing the plight of the Black men and women of America at the time and saluting their contribution to building the country. Laurens protests slavery, adding: "But we'll never be truly free/Until those in bondage have the same rights as you and me" and dreams of creating "the first Black battalion." Writing on this plan in documents of the time, Hamilton insists it's an excellent idea and asserts that "their natural facilities are probably as good as ours" and that they will make better soldiers than the white troops. As he concludes, "I foresee that this project will have to combat much opposition from prejudice and self-interest. The contempt we have been taught to entertain for the blacks makes us fancy many things that are founded neither in reason not experience" (Villegas 62). Though the son of one of South Carolina's most influential planters, Laurens believed passionately in abolition and wrote essays hoping to free American slaves to fight in the Revolution. The South rejected them all. Meanwhile, the show emphasizes his passion, shared with Hamilton, even as the war is won:

> HAMILTON/LAURENS: We'll never be free until we end slavery!
>
> ...
>
> LAURENS: Black and white soldiers wonder alike if this really means freedom
>
> WASHINGTON: Not. Yet. ("Yorktown")

After losing Laurens but winning the Revolution, Hamilton kept trying to free the slaves. Chernow explains: "Hamilton co-founds the first anti-slavery society in New York, The Manumission Society. He's arguably the most consistent abolitionist among the founders, and it's kind of a thread that runs consistently throughout his entire life" (*Alexander Hamilton: American Experience*). Historian Carol Berkin adds: "I think his opposition to slavery is of a piece with his general belief in meritocracy. He says slavery keeps men, who might make major contributions to our society—prevents them from doing that and so it's inefficient. It doesn't let people who have talent use their talents well" (*Alexander Hamilton: American Experience*).

In the musical's first cabinet battle, Hamilton calls Jefferson out on who's really tilling his fields ("We all know who's really doing the planting!"). A third cabinet battle tackled

HAMILTON'S WOMEN

slavery but was cut as it didn't actually reveal much about the characters or move the plot forward. Still, it appears on the mix tape. "This is the stain on our soul and democracy," Hamilton insists (*Hamilton: The Revolution,* 213). He also brings up Sally Hemings, asking provocatively, "How will Thomas Jefferson find his next mistresses?" and more directly describing "All your hemming and hawing, while you're hee-hawing with Sally Hemings." Of course, this moment in the rap battle alludes to his historical character's revealing the scandal. However, in the song, his enemies ask him whether he really wants to bring up the other man's mistress (after his own scandalous behavior), and he capitulates. In the debate, Hamilton and Jefferson are actually more closely aligned than in the other two, both acknowledging that slavery is evil but that they don't have good financial or practical solutions for handling emancipation.

On the other hand, Jefferson's point that "We cannot cure prejudice or righteous, desperate hate," is true as well (212). Washington is uncertain (though a slave owner, he did free his slaves upon his death) but concludes it is too volatile an issue to address, a viewpoint that lays the ground for the later Civil War. As the show ends, Washington bows his head, acknowledging his own culpability here, as Eliza regrets in the final number that Hamilton couldn't do everything he wanted, like end the torture and sale of fellow human beings. In fact, the real Eliza died as the rumbles of the Civil War began, emphasizing how she was one of the few to witness the consequences.

VALERIE ESTELLE FRANKEL

Martha Washington

While Martha Washington does not appear onstage, she's hinted at in Washington's desire to return home and retire—a life he will spend with his wife. Further, this desire for domesticity contrasts with Hamilton and Eliza, as she begs him to make a similar choice in "That Would Be Enough," and Hamilton refuses. Washington's time as general and then president is shown, though Martha (who served beside him in both jobs and helped organize the soldiers' balls of "Helpless" as well) is not only unseen but unmentioned—a sad omission, but one that keeps the story focused on Hamilton and his friends, mentors and adversaries. Nonetheless, the character gets in a quick jibe through the mention that she named her ladykiller tomcat after Hamilton—a historical truth that nods to a joking relationship between them.

More importantly, Martha was actively a mentor and devoted friend for Eliza, paralleling Washington and Hamilton's relationship: "It was her growing friendship with Martha Washington that most inspired her. Martha Washington—with her homespun dresses and quiet modesty—was Eliza's ideal. Eliza had loved the afternoons when she and Martha sat together at camp, chatting quietly over tea and patiently working on their embroidery, a shared passion. Theirs was a friendship that would sustain Eliza more and more in the times ahead of them," Mazzeo explains (82). Martha actually found herself closely tied to the young couple's story. In fact, after Hamilton walked out on Washington and his Revolution, Martha found herself taking over part of his job and making fair copies of her husband's correspondence.

Both Martha and Eliza, aside from being thrust into the

HAMILTON'S WOMEN

public eye, were women devoted to home and family life who somehow made it all work. As their husbands' political careers took off, the relationship continued: "She and Martha Washington, both of whom understood public pressures and how they grew wearing and who shared a love of sober, simple pleasures, passed quiet summer evenings together stitching needlework in the sunset. Martha Washington missed her rural home. Eliza understood her longing. They talked of the Pastures and of Mount Vernon and gardens" (Mazzeo 134).

After the Reynolds Pamphlet, public support from the Washingtons (still influential after their retirement) was essential: Martha Washington invited Eliza out on her social rounds under her considerable protection. "Mrs Washington sends her Love to Mrs Hamilton," Martha wrote in one early morning note. "She intends visiting Mrs Peters this fore noon, if it is agreeable to Mrs H to go with her she will be happy to have company" (Mazzeo 174). Though she and her husband knew the gossip that was circulating and had no reason to doubt that Alexander was cheating on his wife, they publicly supported the couple. When Alexander fell ill, Martha Washington sent over some special bottles of Madeira as a get-well present, and wrote to Eliza, "I am truly glad my Dear Madam to hear Colo. Hamilton is better to day. You have my prayers and warmest wishes for his recovery. I hope you take care of yourself as you know it is necessary for your family," signing off, "your Very affectionate Friend M. Washington" (Mazzeo 174). Her support lasted for all her lifetime.

VALERIE ESTELLE FRANKEL

ABIGAIL ADAMS

John Adams and his wife Abigail likewise both go unseen but are notable presences in the story—Eliza reminds her husband that John Adams spends summers with his family, and King George smirks at the man's lack of presence. Still, for those who know Abigail's reputation as the perfect helpmeet, mother, and patriot—as well as protector of her husband's legacy who kept all his correspondence safe for history—there's a notable echo in Eliza's living presence. Angelica also invokes her with a plan to confront Jefferson and "compel him to include women in the sequel" to the Declaration of Independence, which mirrors Abigail's famous plea that her husband "remember the ladies."

This was a request that he consider the onerous law of coverture—through which daughters were handed from their father to a husband with no rights to their own property. Women could not vote or sign contracts—in the eyes of the law they were nonexistent, with their husbands legally responsible for all their actions and able to jail them, send them to mental institutions, deny them medical care, abuse them, or do anything else they desired. Abigail in fact pleaded, "Do not put such unlimited power in the hands of the Husbands. Remember all Men would be tyrants if they could." However, even as the men held a rebellion based on the principles of representation, none made laws offering this same representation to women. Feminist historian Catherine Allgor suggests that because the Founding Fathers were uncertain whether America would succeed, they were hesitant in this area: "Anxiety over legitimacy made the framers and founding men sensitive to anything that would seem to diminish or challenge their authority. In an age that equated masculinity with authority, that meant anything that made them feel or seem less

112

HAMILTON'S WOMEN

than men" (112). Freeing their wives from this dependence thus was something they speedily dismissed.

In this world of second-class citizens, only Burr seemed to subscribe to true equality—particularly in how he supported his wife's education and then passed this skill on to his daughter. "It is not odd that women respected Burr. He respected them. Perhaps that is why Abigail Adams sought to convince her husband that if either Jefferson or Burr was chosen to replace him in 1800, Burr was to be preferred as "the more bold, daring, and decisive," reports Roger G. Kennedy in his history book *Burr, Hamilton, and Jefferson* (61).

Meanwhile, the cut song "The Adams Administration" actually invoked her more directly. Hamilton blasts Adams in his letter:

> Give my regards to Abigail
> Next time you write about my lack of moral compass
> At least I'm doin' my job up in this rumpus

This apparently references a 1797 letter from John Adams to Abigail Adams: "Hamilton I know to be a proud Spirited, conceited, aspiring Mortal always pretending to Morality, with as debauched Morals as old Franklin who is more his Model than any one I know. As great an Hypocrite as any in the U.S." However, Miranda removed most of the song as this obsession with a character who doesn't appear in the story veered too far off course. Further, he adds that the audience seemed offended by the perceived insult at the immorality of founding mother Abigail Adams. As Miranda explains, "In a workshop reading, this was Hamilton talking smack about Abigail Adams's appearance—something the historical Hamilton never did, but par for the course in hip-hop insults. One look at the audience's cringing reaction and I cut it. *No one* messes with Abigail Adams. We just won't have it" (Miranda 224). Thus, the line was consigned to history.

DOLLEY MADISON

While Eliza is friendly with Mrs. Theodosia Burr in a cut song, her relationship to the various presidents' wives goes unseen. Hamilton gets in a jibe at Jefferson's illicit relationship with Sally Hemings, but no more. However, the history of Dolley Madison and her effect on government of the time is fascinating. Martha Washington had played matchmaker for Dolley and James Madison, as she had for the Hamiltons. She was a dear, supportive friend to each couple.

When Jefferson became president, his wife was dead and his daughter, married and living far away. Burr, his Vice President, was a widower as well, with his own daughter having just married and departed for the South. According to protocol, the president could not host female guests (some of them important dignitaries' wives) without a hostess to invite them in particular. Thus, he turned to the thirty-three-year-old wife of his dear friend James Madison, his Secretary of State. The first dinner held was a success, and she became Jefferson's hostess for social functions, acting somewhat as the defacto chief of staff for his own eight-year presidency before doing so for her husband's. She created the hostess role, not envisioned or described in the Constitution, but necessary for social mores of the time.

When she became First Lady in truth (though the term had not yet been established and she was often known as the "Presidentress"), Dolley likewise set the precedent for an Inaugural Ball and then decorated the interior of the White House, mostly with American furniture and household goods. With all this, she made a permanent impression on the White House for all the generation to come.

Much later, as a presidential widow, she entered history once again when she recruited Eliza to help her raise funds

HAMILTON'S WOMEN

for the Washington Monument. Along with Louisa Adams, widow of John Quincy Adams, they created a women's committee to raise needed funds to commence building. Of course, their fame and appeal as Founding Mothers inspired many to contribute. They gathered enough to begin and held a cornerstone-laying ceremony on July 4, 1848. While the Civil War would delay construction work and the monument would not be completed until 1884, it still stands as a result of their efforts.

THE BULLET

The Bullet, apparently a near-invisible ensemble member who only stands out because of a poof of curls at the top of her head, not only functions like a Greek chorus like the rest of the ensemble but finally embodies the shot that kills Hamilton. Moreover, throughout the show, she plays the part aware of her and Hamilton's final fate and throws in tiny moments because of this. While the rest of the ensemble generally return to the anonymous chorus until their next role, the Bullet never leaves awareness of her role behind. All this subtle storyline elevates her to a real character.

When asked about her role, Ariana DeBose, the original Bullet, explains, "I always know I'm aiming for him—even if the rest of the ensemble members don't. So even if I'm just a lady in a ball gown at a party, there's still a part of my character that knows that *that* moment is going to come." Viewers watching her actions see much more than another ensemble member as she sets her sights on Hamilton throughout his life. In fact, DeBose played the part with such specificity that she became known to Hamilton's social-media-savvy fans as "#thebullet" (Freed).

After "You'll Be Back," she plays a spy receiving a letter, only to have a redcoat snap her neck, making her the first death of the Revolution. Next, in "Stay Alive," she becomes

115

VALERIE ESTELLE FRANKEL

the actual Bullet as she passes Hamilton by during the sound of the gunshot at the song's beginning. Sarah Hollinger, who replaced DeBose as the Bullet in New York, explains that DeBose developed the performance with very particular movements, including forming one of her hands to appear to be holding the bullet. "Your pointer finger and thumb cannot touch, your other three fingers can't move at all," Hollinger says (Freed). "From that moment on, every second she is allowed the audience's full or even partial attention, she becomes a harbinger of death," Phoebe Corde adds in her essay on the Bullet—"The Piece of Foreshadowing in *Hamilton* That Everyone Misses."

> Even when the spotlight is not on her, every moment the Bullet is onstage has significance. Whether it's in "My Shot," when the ensemble unfreezes one by one as Hamilton moves toward them during his first recitation of the "I imagine death so much it feels more like a memory" monologue and the Bullet is the last one to move, her hand still outstretched toward Hamilton as he steps in front of her, or it's in "Ten Duel Commandments," when the ensemble lines up between Hamilton and Burr, singing, "Pick a place to die where it's high and dry," and the Bullet places herself directly at Hamilton's side, the connection between them is already being formed. Knowing that the Bullet is fully aware of the final meeting she and Hamilton are hurtling toward makes the short moment in "Ten Duel Commandments" when Hamilton looks at her lining up beside him, the only time he ever seems to truly see her before his final moments, and the pair stand side by side for numbers six and seven of the Commandments, moving through the choreography in sync, feel hugely significant in a way it never would otherwise. (Corde)

The Bullet's place next to Hamilton during "Ten Duel Commandments" for the line, "Pick a place to die where it's high and dry"—a move that she will replicate when the song is reprised before Hamilton's death—is no accident. The strong vowels even heighten the audience's attention here. In fact, the line emphasizes that when Hamilton does "Pick a place to die where it's high and dry"—choosing the cliffs of New Jersey where his son was shot—he will indeed die there.

As Act One builds to a climax, during "Yorktown," she

HAMILTON'S WOMEN

kills a redcoat with Laurens in South Carolina. They celebrate briefly before she returns to the ensemble and happily shake hands. Of course, it's soon revealed that this was Laurens' last moment onstage, as his final battle ended his life. The bullet's fingerprints are visible here as well. The Bullet and Laurens even exchange a significant glance, that feels as if he realizes that his fate is indeed coming for him.

> That Hamilton, both the man and the musical, are preoccupied with death is no secret: The Founding Father was fascinated by his own mortality ("I imagine death so much it feels just like a memory"), and Miranda wrote that into the central core of his leading man's persona. Similarly, death, and the specifics of Hamilton's, is hinted at in the copious references to shots and gunfire. The Bullet brings that preoccupation onto the stage. (Vincent)

In the Second Act, her brief connections with other characters become even more significant. In "Blow Us All Away," the Bullet gives Philip directions on exactly where to find George Eaker, explaining, "I saw him just up Broadway, couple of blocks. He was going to see a play." Philip follows her directions and challenges Eaker to the duel that will kill him. She has one other spoken line, as one of Burr's supporters in "The Election of 1800," when she says, "I can't believe we're here with him" and flashes Burr a large, hopeful smile. Burr leaves the exchange triumphant, believing he has the election well in hand, only to have Hamilton destroy his future with one public condemnation. With this, he vows revenge. At the start of "Your Obedient Servant," when Burr formally challenges Hamilton, the Bullet actually pulls Hamilton's desk onto the stage and hands him his quill, arranging the challenge and the final duel.

Once she has successfully gotten the pair to pull their guns on each other, she changes into the bullet, approaching Hamilton incredibly slowly throughout his final monologue, coming dangerously close. Halfway through, Hamilton steps directly into her path, turns back and stumbles out of the way. As he frantically repeats, "Rise up, rise up, rise up," she lunges for him, only for another ensemble member to pull her back, keeping her away as Eliza steps in her path. Ariana DeBose explains, "You can look at the final duel in a couple different ways. We're slowing the bullet down to give Hamilton time to say everything he wants to say, or we're saying, 'This is it. It's inevitable. It's happening, so you can stare it right in the face.' There are a lot of different ways to interpret it."

Equally important to that moment in the show is the portrayal of the bullet's perspective. "It's the moment in the duel where time kind of freezes," Hollinger says. "Nothing around Hamilton or Burr is moving. It takes into account his final thoughts. She doesn't know who it's for or who shot her. She only knows she's the bullet" (Freed). Once Hamilton has been shot, she rejoins the ensemble, her mission completed. The moment of silence and stillness has done its job. DeBose adds, "It was really special to create something like that, because it's inspired by a lot of different pieces we've already seen; it's very Matrix-like. I've never seen a moment on stage like it."

THE STORIES THAT AREN'T TOLD: ENSEMBLE

Historian Lyra D. Monteiro objects to the often-repeated idea that the play is "America then, told by America now" as there were certainly Black people in America during the War of Independence. Around fourteen percent of the residents of New York City at the time were Black, most enslaved (62). Monteiro explains that this philosophy "is misleading and actively erases the presence and role of black and brown people in Revolutionary America, as well as before and since"

HAMILTON'S WOMEN

(62). Outside the government buildings, America did look like the *Hamilton* stage. As she adds, the tavern scenes, the Winter's Ball, and the street scenes offer opportunities for slaves to be present. In "The Room Where It Happens," it's inaccurate and dismissive to say "no one else" was there, as slaves would have served dinner (64).

When Jefferson arrives in America, slaves are scrubbing his floor and pushing the very staircase he rides. Their backing up his song obediently suggests King George's courtiers, forced to sing along happily. However, none are given a voice or a chance to say anything on their own behalfs. They are erased from the story.

In fact, as Monteiro points out, no historically Black characters appear onstage (excepting a wordless Sally Hemings). "More blatantly, the play omits the role of Hercules Mulligan's slave Cato, who bravely assisted Mulligan's efforts to spy on the British. In *Hamilton,* Mulligan sings about these accomplishments as if they were his alone" (64). The historical romance novel *The Hamilton Affair,* by contrast, mentions heroes of color like Crispus Attucks. More importantly, it stars the fictional free Black soldier Ajax Manly, whom Hamilton befriends because of the name he shares with his own childhood companion. Later, in Philadelphia, and then New York, Ajax lives as a printer and finally falls in love with a slave, and must fight so their first child does not share his mother's fate. As Eliza grows closer to him, she discovers how to break through the race barriers to love and respect him like family. She pleads with his wife's owners to free her and Eliza's petition is finally granted when they sympathize with her losing Philip. This delightful perspective in the novel emphasizes how whitewashed history often ends up.

In the show, slavery is addressed but often downplayed, and viewers must know their history to realize that Washington's, Madison's, and Eliza's fortunes were based in slavery—not just Jefferson's. Mention is made of Hamilton's work towards abolition (though his founding the New York Manumission Society was something of a different matter—

manumission meant voluntarily freeing one's slaves, as Washington did on his death). Hamilton's childhood among suffering slaves is remarked on in one of the first lines, but not his mother's owning slaves including one assigned to him, or his clerking for slavers to get his self-made education. There's evidence he and Eliza rented them, and Hamilton is on record buying slaves for the Schuylers. Therefore, the show offers a biased view of history as it casts Hamilton and Washington as truly great, as well as likely more anti-slavery than historical documents suggest. This celebration of the founders while sweeping slavery under the rug has many critics concerned. It does not hold the Founding Fathers responsible for holding slaves and does not honor those who suffered through it, or acknowledge these policies' effects on the world today.

Though these complaints have been made a few places, most fans, especially those of color, appreciate Miranda's recasting the story of the Founding Fathers and "putting them back in the narrative," so to speak. "It also feels appropriate that the ultimate dead white men of American history should be portrayed here by men who are not white. The United States was created, exclusively and of necessity, by people who came from other places or their immediate descendants," Ben Brantley writes in a review. Director Thomas Kail explains, "What we're trying to do with the cast and the larger gesture of the show is say here's a group of people that you think you can't relate to. Maybe we can take down some of those barriers and allow a reflection to be truer" (*Hamilton's America*). "It is quite literally taking the history that someone has tried to exclude us from and reclaiming it," says Leslie Odom Jr., Aaron Burr. "We are saying we have the right to tell it too" (Binelli).

Of course, people of color wrote and composed the musical, so they certainly reclaim a voice through the narrative. The question, meanwhile, is whether they do justice to the female characters. Fourth wave feminism is concerned with intersectionality, realizing that different marginalized groups

HAMILTON'S WOMEN

have much in common and should fight to further all their interests together. "At the root of feminism and feminist ethics is the belief that people should be treated with dignity, regardless of their gender. Extended to its natural conclusions, feminism must connect and overlap with anti-racist efforts," Dobrick adds (183). The historical women, of course, make up their own marginalized class, and one that, like the slaves, is often dismissed onstage.

> Who were the women that Hamilton was tomcatting around with or with whom Hercules Mulligan boasted of having "intercourse over four sets of corsets?" Were these upper-class "ladies," or are we to understand that our heroes were exploiting poor women, such as the boardinghouse keeper's daughters or prostitutes who frequented the urban public sphere or military camps? However we are supposed to understand these sexual transactions, Hamilton highlights cavalier attitudes that reflect a masculinist perspective. (Allgor 100-101)

With this, Allgor emphasizes how much women are treated like background players—not just unimportant characters but commodities or victims exploited and dumped—while possibly pregnant or publicly compromised—by the men. This is, in fact, a male story and the women, if not Schuylers or Founding Mothers, are basically window dressing.

At the same time, Lorens tells both men and women to "rise up," adding the line "tell your sister," to join, suggesting it's the women's revolution too. Later, Burr actively campaigns, reminding women to "tell your husbands" to vote for him—though they did not have the vote, he knew they could thus influence the political process.

Moreover, casting women as soldiers alongside the men in battle scenes hints at a rewritten egalitarian past, much like casting white founders as Black actors accomplishes. It also nods to actual women of the Revolution like Molly Pitcher (a nickname given to both Mary Ludwig Hays and Margaret Corbin) who loaded cannons, though none are named in the show. Still, the chorus in their bustling emphasize the lives of ordinary people surrounding the main characters. "Even during solo numbers, we're aware of other people onstage, exhaling the sense of varied and multiple lives contingent upon one another," Brantley concludes.

Women's roles in the story are striking but minimized, as this book has pointed out. "Feminism is about equality in all facets of life. *Hamilton* is a show about storytelling, and so its true feminist triumph is in depicting the ways in which its female characters take on the story in their own way, through adversity and under the circumstances they've been given. Women always have a place, but not necessarily a voice. *Hamilton*'s women carve out space for their own voices and their own stories, in small but meaningful ways," Sarah Halle Corey decides in "The Women of *Hamilton* Are Your New Feminist Sheroes."

Still, in high school productions and in the future, there's opportunity for the parts to be gender-flipped, as many have already noticed. "A gone-viral YouTube clip of #Ham4Ham 1/3/16 with The Ladies of Hamilton features the women actors impersonating the male characters outside the theatre. I think girls in these roles would be sensational and would foreground how little the female characters get to do and how they function in the musical. Like Angelica Schuyler, I'm excited about the sequel," Wolf gushes. In another Ham4Ham show (pre-show performances accompanying the drawing for discount tickets), the three King Georges sang "The Schuyler Sisters," with Goldberry MCing as Aaron Burr, all exploring the scope for nontraditional roles in future.

> Speaking at an event at the Smithsonian Museum of American History in Washington, D.C., Friday, the show's creator and star Lin Manuel Miranda was asked by a fan in the audience if he could ever see women taking on the iconic roles in his musical. "It's a complicated answer," he said. "My only trouble with doing it on Broadway is (music) keys. Because changing keys is a pain. You can actually hear in (his first musical, *In the Heights*) how tough it is just to write a duet for a guy and a girl to sing together. It's a challenge as a writer for them both to sound good. So that's my trouble....That being said, no one's voice is set in high school," he continued. "So I'm totally open to women playing founding fathers once this goes into the world. I can't wait to see

HAMILTON'S WOMEN

> kick-ass women Jeffersons and kickass women Hamiltons once this gets to schools." (Lawler)

"Considering the very, very enthusiastic reaction of the young women in the crowd, that seems like something that could happen," Lawler concludes.

The mix tape also allowed more women's voices into the show: Jill Scott, Andra Day, Ashanti, Queen Latifah, and Alicia Keys filled in for Eliza, Angelica, and Maria, while Dessa added the cut song "Congratulations." (They also adapted this as they wished with Ashanti pointedly rejecting Angelica's desire to share Hamilton and Jill Scott claiming more agency with "Say Yes to This.") A few other songs are taken over by women, with Regina Spektor offering a loving "Dear Theodosia" and Kelly Clarkson soulfully taking over Hamilton's as well as Angelica's part in "It's Quiet Uptown."

Miranda, meanwhile, has been applauded for his sensitivity to women's issues. He raised money for Hillary Clinton in 2016. Three weeks after Vice-President-Elect Pense attended *Hamilton* and the actors implored him to represent all Americans, Miranda partnered with Prizeo to raffle off *Hamilton* tickets to those who donated to Planned Parenthood, where his mother, Luz Townes-Miranda, serves on the board of the national political action division.

VALERIE ESTELLE FRANKEL

Conclusion

So how do the women of *Hamilton* rate? Their cultural influence must be weighed alongside their roles in the story. Thanks to the musical, teens are singing along and dressing as the sisters for Halloween or at comic-cons. Though the historic Schuyler sisters were white, many teens of color adore having assertive, musical heroines who look like themselves. There's also the beautiful songs and snappy raps that many play nonstop.

Onstage, the four female characters are seen through Hamilton's eyes and only appear in the context of their relationships with him, from the first song to the last. Angelica's wit and political savvy and Eliza's assertive heroism both are used to support their beloved Alexander, both during his life and after his death. From a feminist perspective, this male-centric narrative is far from perfect.

Nonetheless, their accomplishments are true to history and to the characters they play. Both women thus offer a message that, even in a setting of limited options, they each seized life and claimed positions that influenced history. Even if the men were the ones dominating the story, they could still reclaim the narrative and tell it their way.

VALERIE ESTELLE FRANKEL

Appendix

VALERIE ESTELLE FRANKEL

HAMILTON'S WOMEN

Songs

Hamilton Album: Act 1
Alexander Hamilton
Aaron Burr, Sir
My Shot
Story Of Tonight
Schuyler Sisters
Farmer Refuted
You'll Be Back
Right Hand Man
A Winter's Ball
Helpless
Satisfied
The Story of Tonight (Reprise)
Wait For It
Stay Alive
Ten Duel Commandments
Meet Me Inside
That Would Be Enough
Guns and Ships
History Has Its Eyes On You
Yorktown (The World Turned Upside Down)
What Comes Next
Dear Theodosia
Non-Stop

Hamilton Album: Act 2
What'd I Miss
Cabinet Battle #1
Take A Break
Say No To This
Room Where It Happens
Schuyler Defeated
Cabinet Battle #2
Washington On Your Side
One Last Time

VALERIE ESTELLE FRANKEL

I Know Him
The Adams Administration
We Know
Hurricane
The Reynolds Pamphlet
Burn
Blow Us All Away
Stay Alive (Reprise)
It's Quiet Uptown
Election of 1800
Your Obedient Servant
Best of Wives and Best of Women
The World Was Wide Enough
Who Lives, Who Dies, Who Tells Your Story

ORIGINAL CAST AND CREATORS 2015-2016

The world premiere of "Hamilton" was presented in New York in February 2015 by The Public Theater (Off-Broadway). It moved to the Richard Rodgers Theatre on Broadway 8/06/2015.

Book by Lin-Manuel Miranda; Music by Lin-Manuel Miranda; Lyrics by Lin-Manuel Miranda
Inspired by the book *Alexander Hamilton* by Ron Chernow
Music Direction and Orchestrations by Alex Lacamoire; Arrangements by Alex Lacamoire and Lin-Manuel Miranda
Directed by Thomas Kail
Choreography by Andy Blankenbuehler
Scenic Design by David Korins
Costume Design by Paul Tazewell
Lighting Design by Howell Binkley
Sound Design by Nevin Steinberg
Hair and Wig Design by Charles G. LaPointe

Cast
Alexander Hamilton...Lin-Manuel Miranda
Aaron Burr...Leslie Odom, Jr.
Eliza Schuyler Hamilton...Phillipa Soo
Angelica Schuyler...Renée Elise Goldsberry
Marquis de Lafayette/Thomas Jefferson... Daveed Diggs
George Washington...Christopher Jackson
King George III...Brian d'Arcy James (Off-Broadway)
King George III...Jonathan Groff (Broadway)
John Laurens / Philip Hamilton...Anthony Ramos
Peggy Schuyler / Maria Reynolds...Jasmine Cephas Jones
Hercules Mulligan / James Madison...Okieriete Onaodowan

WORKS CITED

Adams, William Howard. *The Paris Years of Thomas Jefferson.* Yale University Press, 1997.

Adelman, Joseph M. "Who Tells Your Story: *Hamilton* as a People's History." *Historians on Hamilton How a Blockbuster Musical Is Restaging America's Past,* edited by Renee C. Romano and Claire Bond Potter. Rutgers, 2019, pp. 277-296.

Alexander Hamilton: American Experience, written by Ronald Blumer, produced and directed by Muffie Meyer, PBS, 2007.
http://www.pbs.org/wgbh/amex/hamilton/filmmore/pt.html.

Allgor, Catherine. "'Remember....I'm Your Man': Masculinity, Marriage, and Gender in *Hamilton." Historians on Hamilton How a Blockbuster Musical Is Restaging America's Past,* edited by Renee C. Romano and Claire Bond Potter. Rutgers, 2019, pp. 94-115.

Baskervill, Bill. "Newly Discovered Jefferson Letters Hint of Loneliness and Love". *Los Angeles Times* 21 July 1996.

Berkin, Carol. Revolutionary Mothers: Women in the Struggle for America's Independence. Random House, 2005.

Brands, H.W. The Heartbreak of Aaron Burr. Anchor Books, 2012.

Binelli, Mark. "Hamilton Mania." *Rolling Stone,* vol. 1263, 2016, pp. 36. MasterFILE Premier.

Brantley, Ben. "Review: In 'Hamilton,' Lin-Manuel Miranda Forges Democracy Through Rap." *The New York Times,* 17 Feb 2015
https://www.nytimes.com/2015/02/18/theater/review-in-hamilton-lin-manuel-miranda-forges-democracy-through-rap.html.

Chernow, Ron. *Alexander Hamilton.* Penguin Books, 2005.

Corde, Phoebe. "The Piece of Foreshadowing in *Hamilton*

That Everyone Misses." *Odyssey,* 19 Sept 2016. https://www.theodysseyonline.com/piece-foreshadowing-hamilton-misses.

Corey, Sarah Halle. "The Women of *Hamilton* Are Your New Feminist Sheroes." *Hello Flo,* 6 Jan 2016 http://helloflo.com/the-women-of-hamilton-are-your-new-feminist-sheroes.

DeBose, Ariana. Interview by Kelly d'Amboise, *The Great Discontent,* 9 Jun 2016 https://thegreatdiscontent.com/interview/ariana-debose

DiGiacomo, Frank. "*Hamilton*'s Lin-Manuel Miranda on Finding Originality, Racial Politics (and Why Trump Should See His Show)" *Hollywood Reporter,* 12 Aug. 2015. http://www.hollywoodreporter.com/features/hamiltons-lin-manuel-miranda-finding-814657.

Dreamcatcher. "All Deleted Songs from *Hamilton.*" 6 Dec. 2016. https://www.youtube.com/watch?v=EZkANYGycNU.

Dobrick, Alison. "To the Revelation!" *Hamilton and Philosophy: Revolutionary Thinking,* edited by Aaron Rabinowitz and Robert Arp. Open Court, 2017, pp. **177-183.**

Eggert, Jessica. "'Satisfied' Lyrics: Reviews and Meaning Behind *Hamilton* Musical Song." *Mic.com,* 22 Oct. 2015. https://mic.com/articles/127218/satisfied-lyrics-reviews-and-meaning-behind-hamilton-musical-song.

"Elizabeth Hamilton (1757–1854)." *American Experience.* PBS. https://www.pbs.org/wgbh/americanexperience/features/hamilton-elizabeth-hamilton-1757-1854/

Elliott, L.M. "Who Were the Schuyler Sisters? Fact and Fiction in *Hamilton*" *DC Metro Theater Arts,* 10 July 2018 https://dcmetrotheaterarts.com/2018/07/10/who-were-the-schuyler-sisters-fact-and-fiction-in-hamilton.

"Esther Edwards Burr," *Women's History Blog,* Nov 2008. http://www.womenhistoryblog.com/2008/11/esther-edwards-burr-1754.html

Fleming, Thomas. The Intimate Lives of the Founding Fathers. Smithsonian, 2009.

Frankel, Valerie Estelle. *Who Tells Your Story*. LitCrit, 2016.

Freed, Benjamin. "Actress and Dancer from Washington to Play "#thebullet" in Hamilton." *Washingtonian,* 7 July 2016.
https://www.washingtonian.com/2016/07/07/actress-grew-woodbridge-play-bullet-hamilton

Grady, Constance. "How the Women of *Hamilton* Are Changing Broadway." *Vox,* 8 Aug 2016,
https://www.vox.com/2016/2/23/11058702/hamilton-angelica-eliza-schuyler-love-triangle

Green, Jesse. "Theater Review: Is *Hamilton* Even Better Than It Was?" *Vulture,* 6 Aug 2015.
https://www.vulture.com/2015/08/theater-review-hamilton.html

Hamilton's America. PBS, 21 Oct. 2016.

Harris, Leslie M. "The Greatest City in the World? Slavery in New York in the Age of Hamilton." *Historians on Hamilton How a Blockbuster Musical Is Restaging America's Past,* edited by Renee C. Romano and Claire Bond Potter. Rutgers, 2019, pp. 71-93.

Humphreys, Mary Gay. *Catherine Schuyler.* C. Scribner's Sons, 1897. *Archive.org*
https://archive.org/details/catherineschuyl01humpgoog/page/n96

Isenberg, Nancy. *Fallen Founder: The Life of Aaron Burr.* Penguin Books, 2007.

Jacob, Mark and Stephen Case. Treacherous Beauty: Peggy Shippen, the Woman behind Benedict Arnold's Plot to Betray America. Lyons, 2012.

Kennedy, Roger G. Burr, Hamilton, and Jefferson: A Study in Character. Oxford University Press, 2000.

Lawler, Kelly. "*Hamilton* Creator Would Love Women to Play the Founding Fathers." *USA Today,* 13 Nov 2015.
https://www.usatoday.com/story/life/theater/2015/11/13/hamilton-musical-lin-manuel-miranda-women-founding-
fa-

thers/75708076/?utm_source=feedblitz&utm_medium=
FeedBlitzRss&utm_campaign=usatoday-lifetopstories

Mazzeo, Tilar J. Eliza Hamilton: The Extraordinary Life and Times of the Wife of Alexander Hamilton. Gallery Books, 2018.

Meares, Hadley. "The Dramatic Life and Mysterious Death of Theodosia Burr." *Atlas Obscura*, 7 Oct 2016. https://www.atlasobscura.com/articles/the-dramatic-life-and-mysterious-death-of-theodosia-burr.

Monteiro, Lyra D. "Race-Conscious Casting and the Erasure of the Black Past in *Hamilton." Historians on Hamilton How a Blockbuster Musical Is Restaging America's Past,* edited by Renee C. Romano and Claire Bond Potter. Rutgers, 2019, pp. 58-70.

Purcell, Carey. *"Hamilton* Star Renée Elise Goldsberry on Bringing Feminism and Diversity to Broadway: BUST Interview." *Bust,* 2019. https://bust.com/music/16238-hamilton-star-renee-elise-goldsberry-on-bringing-feminism-and-diversity-to-broadway-bust-interview.html

Ross, Benjamin. "Eliza Hamilton, Buddhist Master." *Hamilton and Philosophy: Revolutionary Thinking,* edited by Aaron Rabinowitz and Robert Arp. Open Court, 2017, pp. 115-121.

Schulman, Michael. "The Women of *Hamilton." The New Yorker,* 6 Aug 2015. https://www.newyorker.com/culture/cultural-comment/the-women-of-hamilton

Semigran, Aly. "The Women of *Hamilton*: Making Herstory on Broadway." *Amy Smart Girl,* 7 Mar2016 https://amysmartgirls.com/the-women-of-hamilton-making-herstory-on-broadway-e507820a319

Timm, Chad William. "History Has Its Eyes on You." *Hamilton and Philosophy: Revolutionary Thinking,* edited by Aaron Rabinowitz and Robert Arp. Open Court, 2017, pp. 197-207.

Villegas, Christina G. *Documents Decoded: Alexander Hamilton.* ABC-CLIO, 2018.

Vincent, Alice. "The Bullet: Why Hamilton's 'Secret' Charac-

VALERIE ESTELLE FRANKEL

ter Is its Most Important." *The Telegraph*, 16 Jan 2018. https://www.telegraph.co.uk/theatre/what-to-see/bullet-hamiltons-secret-character-important

Wible, Andy. "One Eye on the Future." *Hamilton and Philosophy: Revolutionary Thinking,* edited by Aaron Rabinowitz and Robert Arp. Open Court, 2017, pp. 95-103.

Wolf, Stacy. "Hamilton." *The Feminist Spectator,* 24 Feb 2016. http://feministspectator.princeton.edu/2016/02/24/hamilton.

About the Author

Valerie Estelle Frankel is the author of many books on pop culture, including *Doctor Who – The What, Where, and How*, *Sherlock: Every Canon Reference You May Have Missed in BBC's Series 1-3*, and *How Game of Thrones Will End*. Many of her books focus on women's roles in fiction, from her heroine's journey guides *From Girl to Goddess* and *Buffy and the Heroine's Journey* to books like *Women in Game of Thrones* and *The Many Faces of Katniss Everdeen*. Once a lecturer at San Jose State University, she's a frequent speaker at conferences. Come explore her research at www.vefrankel.com.

CPSIA information can be obtained
at www.ICGtesting.com
Printed in the USA
LVHW100941110422
715875LV00003B/28